ISLAMIC AFRICA

ISLAMIC AFRICA

VOLUME 2, ISSUE 1 SPRING 2011

Northwestern University Press
Evanston, Illinois

www.islamicafricajournal.org

Scope and Mission: *Islamic Africa* is a peer-reviewed, multidisciplinary, academic journal published by Northwestern University Press in collaboration with the Institute for the Study of Islamic Thought in Africa (ISITA), based at Northwestern University, Evanston, Illinois. The journal incorporates *Sudanic Africa,* retaining its focus on historical sources, bibliographies, and methodologies. *Islamic Africa* promotes interaction between scholars of Islam and Africa across all continents and across historical periods. The journal welcomes papers from the humanities and the social sciences on any aspect of Islam and Muslim life pertaining to Africa, or originating from the African continent.

Communications concerning manuscripts and editorial matters should be addressed to Prof. M. Sani Umar, Editor, *Islamic Africa,* Northwestern University Press, 629 Noyes Street, Evanston, IL 60208 (USA); islamicafrica@northwestern.edu. For information about submitting manuscripts, see www.islamicafricajournal.org.

Concerning advertising and subscriptions, address the Managing Editor, Gianna F. Mosser, Northwestern University Press, 629 Noyes Street, Evanston, IL 60208 (USA); islamicafrica@northwestern.edu. Electronic subscriptions can be purchased for institutions ($125) and individuals ($75) by visiting www.islamicafricajournal.org.

 ISSN 2154-0993.

Northwestern University Press acknowledges Marianne Jankowski for the interior design and Ahmad Faris for the journal logo. The copy editor for this issue was Paul Mendelson.

Islamic Africa **Electronic Journal**
Volume 2, Issue 1
Spring 2011

THE PRESERVATION OF ANCIENT ARABIC MANUSCRIPTS: A REFLECTION ON SOME SELECTED PUBLIC REPOSITORIES IN NORTHERN NIGERIA

Salisu Bala
(Arewa House, Centre for Historical Documentation and Research, Ahmadu Bello University, Nigeria)
DOI: 10.5192/21540993020101

ABSTRACT

The three repositories covered by this paper, the Arewa House Arabic Manuscript repository, the National Jos Museum Arabic Manuscript Collection, and the Gidan Dan Hausa Arabic Manuscripts Collection in Kano, maintain great collections of ancient Arabic manuscripts on diverse subjects. The repositories are in jeopardy due to poor storage systems, lack of capacity building on the part of the staff, and above all laxity on the part of policy makers. The question of procuring and preserving Nigerian Arabic manuscripts for proper utilization by researchers has been a major source of concern to both Nigerian and foreign scholars in the last fifty years or so. Although a lot of progress has been made in this regard since the pioneering days of Professors Abdullahi Smith, K. O. Dike, Murray Last, and others, the three Arabic manuscript repositories covered by this study continue to function in bad conditions, ranging from a lack of paper conservation supplies, poor storage systems, and a complete absence of digitization equipment for proper archiving. However, there is now a definite consensus among researchers and other stakeholders in this field on the urgency of the matter and, happily, a decisive change of attitude towards the fate of the Arabic / Ajami *Manuscripts in most of the repositories of northern Nigeria. A spate of conferences and workshops were organized in quick succession in the last two years and an impressive number of research publications were presented for serious discussions on virtually all aspects of the problems facing the Arabic manuscripts repositories.*

Islamic Africa, VOL. 2, NO. 1, 2011. ISSN 2154-0993. www.islamicafricajournal.org

Introduction

Nigeria's ancient Arabic manuscript collections represent important sources of its intellectual tradition and its history. These manuscripts, especially those produced by indigenous scholars, have greatly aided our understanding of traditions of Islamic learning and the dynamics of intellectual discourses in the West African subregion. Despite the importance of these manuscripts, however, scant attention is being paid to their collection, management, and preservation, and the utilization of the knowledge that is contained therein. Moreover, the repositories that house these valuable documents have not received attention by successive governments at all levels. This has led to the deterioration of the various centers as well as the dilapidation of the manuscripts. This short essay highlights the poor condition of three Arabic manuscript collections: those at the National Museum in Jos, the Arewa House in Kaduna, and the Gidan Dan Hausa History and Culture Bureau in Kano.

The introduction and establishment of Islam in northern Nigeria was the foundation for the production of Arabic manuscripts as well as the development of scholarship in the area, as amply documented by several historians (Mustapha 1987; Zaharadeen 2001; Palmer 1968; Hunwick 1995; Bunza 2006). But most of the present-day collections of Arabic manuscripts, like those of the University of Ibadan, Jos Museum, and the National Archives in Kaduna, were developed during the late colonial period and early independence, from 1957 to 1967. The National Archives in Kaduna collected more than 5,000 Arabic manuscripts from 14 provinces of northern Nigeria, including Kaduna Capital Territory (Usman, A.B., NAK, 2/8/72). In the period from 1959 to the mid-1960s, Abdullahi Smith, M. Hisket, M. A. Alhaj, and Professor Murray Last traversed various provinces in northern Nigeria to collect Arabic manuscripts that were then microfilmed and stored at the University of Ibadan. Subsequently, microfilm copies of 528 manuscripts were brought to Ahmadu Bello University, Zaria, where the Northern History Research Scheme was established in 1964. Up to 1967 the successes recorded in the collection of Arabic manuscripts in northern Nigeria were the result of joint efforts between Ahmadu Bello University and the University of Ibadan.

There are many repositories of ancient Arabic manuscripts in northern Nigeria, and most of them face many problems, including preservation and conservation. The repositories can be divided into two basic types: private and public. Private repositories containing thousands of manuscripts are scattered all over the region. Examples of private repositories include the library of the late Waziri Junaidu of Sokoto, the Sheikh Yahuza Islamic foundation in Zaria, the Sheikh Umar Sanda Islamic Library, and the Sheikh Abubakar Atiku Islamic Centre in Kano. The second type of repository consists of ones in public institutions under the care of universities and the National Archive of Nigeria, such as the Centre for Historical Documentation and Research at Ahmadu Bello University (Arewa House in Kaduna), the National Museum in Jos, the National Archives in Kaduna, the Center for Trans-Saharan Studies of the University of Maiduguri, the Waziri Junaidu History Bureau of Sokoto State, and the Gidan Dan Hausa in Kano. This essay focuses on the problems confronting public collections of Arabic manuscripts in Nigeria.

The National Museum's Arabic Manuscript Collection in Jos

The National Museum in Jos houses a collection of ancient Arabic and *Ajami* manuscripts. Established in 1952 on a wide expanse of land in Jos by the Federal Department of Antiquities during the colonial era, the National Museum has different sections, such as pottery, Museum of Traditional Nigerian Architecture, Museum Library, National Centre for Museum Studies, the Bight of Benin Restaurant (a model of a Benin nobleman's house), as well as a zoo (Bodam 2009).

The museum annually attracts thousands of tourists as well as Nigerian and foreign scholars. It is rich in many respects and delightful to behold. The Arabic manuscript collection was based on the work of Dr. A. H. Bivar (1968) and Mallam Muntaqa Coomasie. It contains manuscripts written by scholars in Nigeria from the sixteenth to the twentieth centuries (Muhammad 1976), and also has valuable printed Arabic books. The manuscripts were written in the Arabic language and in *Ajami* (Hausa or other local languages written in Arabic letters). The Arabic manuscripts are kept in four open shelves, while 438 printed Arabic books occupy two other shelves. There are also some valuable historical records of the colonial period and early editions of reference materials. The Jos Museum Library started collecting Arabic manuscripts from traditional Islamic scholars in 1958 and has about 1,500 manuscripts in its holdings (Oseni 2009). Only 700 have been fully catalogued, but all items were listed with brief explanations. In 1987 the then director general of the National Commission for Museums and Monuments, Professor A. M. Obayemi, requested Professor Zakariyau Oseni of the Department of Arabic, University of Ibadan, to examine the manuscripts and suggest a reclassification and possible ways and methods of preserving them. The place was then on the verge of collapse due to lack of proper handling. The reclassification of the manuscripts was achieved through the introduction of new code numbers of JM/AMs (i.e., Jos Museum/Arabic Manuscripts).

Arewa House Arabic Manuscript Repository

Arewa House is the Center for Historical Documentation and Research of Ahmadu Bello University, the premier university in northern Nigeria. The center is located in Kaduna at the buildings that used to house the office complex of the defunct Northern regional government. Following its establishment in the 1970s, the founding director, Professor Abdullahi Smith, initiated many programs for the procurement, preservation, and content analysis of Arabic manuscripts in northern Nigeria. There were many photographs, microfilms, and few copies of original manuscripts procured during his time. To date, Arewa House has about 1,400 original manuscripts from four different private collections deposited in its archives. The following brief descriptions highlight some of the problems associated with the collections.

Modibbo Ahmadu Fufure Collection

This collection belonged to the late Modibbo Ahmadu Fufure of Yola (1889–1960). It contains about 600 copies of manuscripts, of which 370 have been catalogued so far. They bear various titles, as they were inherited from his great-grandfathers across several generations. Modibbo Ahmadu was born in Fufure, Adamawa Emirate, to Alkali Muhammadu Fufure. His ancestors migrated from Ngazargamu and then to Kukawa before moving to Dikkwa, all in Borno. They settled at Ribadu, and then at Fufure, before they finally moved to Yola, the headquarters of Adamawa Emirate. Modibbo Ahmadu was introduced to Islamic education early in life by his father. Later, he was taught by renowned scholars in Adamawa, such as Modibbo Hammadu, son of Alkalli Hamman-joda, perhaps the most remarkable Islamic judge in the history of Adamawa Emirate, who studied in the Middle East and taught for some time at Al-Azhar University in Egypt. Having passed through these great Islamic scholars, Modibbo Ahmadu became very versatile in various fields of Islamic learning, including *fiqh, tafsīr, Ḥadīth,* as well as Arabic grammar, logic, poetry, literature, astronomy, mathematics, and medicine.

In January 1917 Modibbo Ahmadu was first appointed by the Adamawa

Native Authority as *malamin kasa* (district scribe) in Wuro Marafa of Vere District. In 1935 he began his judicial career as *alkalin* (judge) in Ribadu/Fufore, Jada, and was then promoted to the Grand Khadi Court in Yola as the grand mufti under his teacher, Modibbo Mahmudu. Thereafter, he worked under some notable *alkalis* like Hamidu and Hamman Gabdo in Yola before he was himself appointed the grand khadi (*alkalin alkalai*) of Adamawa Province in 1953, which coincided with the installation of Alhaji Aliyu Musdafa as the eleventh *lamido* of Adamawa.

Apart from his services with the Adamawa Native Authority from 1917 to 1957, Modibbo Ahmadu's greatest achievement was the training of notable Islamic scholars in Adamawa and Cameroon, including Modibbo Umaru Ngaundare and Modibbo Barkindo (both of whom served as the imam of Yola Central Mosque), Modibbo Ibrahim *Alkalin* Ngaundare, and the *lamido* of Adamawa, Alhaji Aliyu Musdafa. Modibbo Ahmadu died in 1960, and is widely remembered as an honest and pious Islamic judge and scholar whose thoughts, words, and deeds were guided by the dictates of the Holy Qurʾan.

The collection is the largest of its kind so far recovered in Adamawa Emirate. It contains many items bearing the finest artistic illuminations and calligraphy in a variety of scripts, and it is also very diverse in terms of the subjects it contains, ranging from various Islamic religious texts, prayers, and sermons to philosophy, ethics and politics, biographies, history, geographical works, grammar, lexicography and philology of Arabic, Fulfulde and Hausa, anthologies of poetry and prose, alchemy, astronomy, traditional medicine, traditional pharmacy, and a large body of correspondence on Mahdism, etc. This outstanding collection representing the long history of Islamic learning and its rich intellectual traditions is now accessible to the public in the Arewa House Archives at Kaduna (Musa 2009).

Sheikh Ahmad Arabi Jos Collection

This collection contains 156 copies of handwritten manuscripts, including volumes of *Ḥadīth* and *fiqh* works. Sheikh Ahmad Arabi of Jos (1910–1973), the original owner of this collection, was born in Nafada in the present Gombe State. He pursued his elementary schooling in Dukku, after which he worked briefly as a court scribe. Sheikh Arabi later moved to Jos where he continued his Islamic education under his uncle, the *alkalin* of Jos, Mallam Abubakar. He was appointed an Arabic teacher at Jos Native Authority Elementary School. Arabi's search for knowledge took him to the famous School for Arabic Studies at Kano, after which he became a teacher there. He was called back by the Jos Native Authority in 1950. In 1947 he founded the *Islamiyya Nizamiyyah* School in Jos. He was appointed as the deputy grand *khadi* for the defunct Benue Plateau and North Eastern states, and chairman of the Benue Plateau State's Muslim Pilgrims Welfare Board. He died in 1973 at the age of 63 (Musa 2008).

Most of the Arabic manuscripts in this collection are written in *naskh* script, but some are written in *kufic* script. The *naskh* has some Maghrib style, especially the curved lettering and the placement of dots above *qāf* and *fāʾ*. The letters and vowels are in different colors. Special reeds were used in writing the older manuscripts, while the new ones are written with modern fountain pens. The paper is of various kinds, watermarks indicating their European manufacturers. The catalogue for this collection adopts the spelling of author and titles of their works as given in each manuscript. It was rather difficult to identify authors' names in the case of manuscripts missing the first pages.

Mallam Musa Ganan Daji Jos Manuscript Collection

The owner of this collection was a scholar and trader who travelled far and wide in Nigeria seeking knowledge and trading. Although originally from the Nupeland in the present Niger State, he finally settled in a village north of Jos. Mallam Musa Ganan Daji collected more than 220 copies of original Arabic and *Ajami* manuscripts written in the nineteenth and twentieth centuries on various Islamic subjects such as interpretation of the Qurʾan and Sufism, as well as astrology and poetry.

Mallam Iliyasu Dalhat Katsina Collection

This collection has about thirty copies of original manuscripts written in the period from the eighteenth to the twentieth centuries. It belonged to Mallam Musa Iliyasu Dalhat of Katsina State. The collection contains items on Sufism, Islamic law, and theology. Arewa House purchased the collection from Mallam Iliyasu Katsina in May 2009, making it accessible to researchers.

Gidan Dan Hausa Arabic Manuscript Collection

Gidan Dan Hausa is the first place that the Kano state government allocated to its newly created Archive Division in 1973. The archival collection was initially housed in different places before it was transferred to its present location in the Nassarawa quarters just outside of the old city of Kano. Some of the items deteriorated because of the poor conditions they were kept in at different locations. The collection is currently under the administrative control of the Kano State History and Culture Bureau established in 1987 to replace the old Kano State Arts Council. Since its establishment, the Kano State Archive Division has been moved to more than six different locations, with the building in one location collapsing during the rainy season, causing severe damage to the items in the collection. Even the present building housing the collection in its "permanent site" does not meet the standard requirements of archival storage.

It is not possible to give the precise number of the Arabic and *Ajami* manuscripts in this collection, mainly due to damage caused to some of the manuscripts in the course of their movements to different locations. By 1988, items in the collection stood at 2,000 official government files, annual reports, gazettes, and assessment reports from the colonial period, while 200 items were Arabic manuscripts. By 1998 the collection had reached 2,391 items, of which 291 were Arabic manuscripts that include handwritten copies of the Qurʾan, works on Islamic theology, jurisprudence, history, and the writings of the leaders of the Sokoto jihad.

Problems of Preservation in the Selected Public Repositories

The present conditions of Arabic manuscripts collections, especially in the Jos Museum Library and Gidan Dan Hausa, are very poor because they are held in buildings that provide anything but protection. These buildings are made of cast concrete or cement block construction, which under tropical conditions absorb a lot of heat with no proper ventilation. Moreover, the roof in the Jos collection is generally flat and hence is full of leaks during the rainy season, which directly affects the manuscripts. As Biddle noted when she visited the repository:

> Today, most of our cherished documentary resources are either totally destroyed or in extreme jeopardy. Although there has been a measure of success in the preservation of the built and natural heritage, there has been no parallel development on a national scale for collections of art, history, literature, information and science housed in our museums, galleries, libraries, archives and associated organizations and private collections held by individuals and corporations. (Biddle 2008)

Apart from the poor condition of the buildings, office equipment is old, worn out, and in desperate need of replacement. Arewa House has now succeeded in securing a new archive where the manuscripts are kept, but the manuscript collection in Kano is stored in environmental conditions that don't support their long-term preservation. The temperature variation ranges between 10.5° and 33.4°C. The excessive heat, high level of humidity in the wet season, heavy dust, and the use of materials that are palatable to insects by the original owners of the manuscripts contribute to molding and severe insect attacks (Plenderleith 1971). To compound the problem further, the staffing of the repository is also very unsatisfactory both in terms of quality and quantity. The staff members generally lack expertise and have very little idea of modern techniques of handling the problems of preservation (Batiste 2007; Biddle 2008). Moreover, there is a chronic shortage of staff arising from deaths and retirements, a problem compounded by lack of paper conservation laboratories.

Conclusion

The numerous problems confronting the collections of Arabic manuscripts in Nigeria require serious attention. The relevant governmental authorities as well as private philanthropists and donors need to provide sufficient funds to establish conservation and preservation laboratories with modern equipment, and provide the necessary training for people to take constant care of the manuscripts. There is also an urgent need to renovate the buildings with appropriate measures taken for the safe storage of the items in the collections, some of which have already been damaged. More helpful catalogues are needed for all the collections so that researchers can easily identify the titles they need to consult without having to go through individual items in each collection. There is the need to organize series of workshops for local religious scholars and all the people involved with manuscript management in order to sensitize them to the importance of preserving these rare, unique, and fragile documents and promote their increased access and use. The individual owners of private collections of manuscripts also need assistance with equipment and tools for preservation. While helping them to keep their collections in good condition, assisting them with these items will also build confidence that enhances their willingness to give access to researchers who need to consult these precious manuscripts. Finally, several scholars have emphasized the need to translate, edit, and analyze the contents of the Arabic manuscripts into English and other local or foreign languages. It is encouraging that Arewa

House has already published collections of papers presented at the conferences it organized on the rich intellectual heritage of Islamic learning in Nigeria.

References

Batiste, A. D. 2007. *Report of a Survey Tour to Northern Nigeria: The State of Arabic Manuscript Collections in Nigeria.* Washington, D.C.: Library of Congress.

Biddle, M. April 2008. *Conservation In a Box: A Primer of Basic Paper Conservation Procedures and Treatments.* Middletown, Conn.: Wesleyan University Library.

———. 2008. *Saving Nigeria's Islamic Manuscript Heritage.* Middletown, Conn.: Wesleyan University Library.

Bivar, A. D. H. 1968. "The Arabic Calligraphy of West Africa." *African Language Review* 7:3–15.

Bodam, R. 2009. "The State of Public and Private Arabic Manuscripts Collections in Jos Plateau State of Nigeria." A paper presented at a two-day National Conference on Exploring Nigeria's Arabic/Ajami Manuscript Resources for the Development of New Knowledge in Nigeria. May 7–8, 2009, Arewa House, Kaduna, Nigeria.

Bunza, U. M. "An Overview of Arabic Medicinal Manuscripts of the Sokoto Caliphate." Paper presented at the Stakeholders Forum organized by the Federal Ministry of Culture, Tourism, and National Orientation. Abuja, Nigeria, October 26–29, 2008.

Hunwick J. O., ed. 1995. *Arabic Literature of Africa 2: The Writings of Central Sudanic Africa.* Leiden: E.J. Brill and New York: Koln.

Ikara, B. 1991. Brochure for the Transformations of Arewa House, Kaduna. Printed by the director, Printing Services, Kaduna.

Muhammad, A. 1976. "A Hausa Scholar-Trader and His Library Collection: The Case Study of Umar Falke of Kano Nigeria." Unpublished Ph.D. thesis, Department of Religious Studies, Northwestern University, Evanston, Ill.

Musa, M. T. "Preservation and Conservation of Arabic and Islamic Manuscripts: A Case for the Sokoto Jihad Literature." Paper presented at National Conference on Exploring Nigeria's Arabic/*Ajami* Manuscripts Resources for the Development of New Knowledge, 2009.

Musa, S. K. "Problems and Prospects of Arabic/*Ajami* Resources for the Development of New Knowledge in Nigeria." Paper presented at National Training Workshop for the Conservation of Arabic Manuscripts in Nigeria.

Arewa House, Centre for Historical Documentation and Research, Nigeria, Technical Workshop Series, 2008.

Mustafa, A. 1987. "The Contribution of Sayfawa ʿUlamaʾ to the Study of Islam c. 1086–1846." Unpublished Ph.D. thesis, Department of Islamic Studies, Bayero University, Kano, Nigeria.

Oseni, Z. 2009. "Arabic Manuscripts in the National Museum at Jos and Their Potentials for the Advancement of Knowledge." A paper presented at a two-day National Conference on Exploring Nigeria's Arabic/Ajami Manuscript Resources for the Development of New Knowledge in Nigeria. Arewa House, Kaduna, Nigeria.

Palmer, H. R. 1928. "Kano Chronicle," in *Sudanese Memoirs, Being Mainly Translation of a Number of Arabic Manuscripts Relating to the Central and Western Sudan*. New York: Negro Universities Press.

Plenderleith, H. J. 1971. *The Conservation of Antiquities and Works of Art: Treatment, Repair, and Restoration.* London: Oxford University Press.

Zaharadeen, S. "Arabic Manuscript Resources in the Sokoto Caliphate." Keynote address, International Conference on the Problems and Prospects of Arabic Manuscripts in Nigeria. Arewa House, Centre for Historical Documentation and Research, Nigeria, 2010.

Archival Conservation Documents

HN. HNNP/7th Meetings: Arewa House, History of Northern Nigeria Project 1970–1971.

———. Arewa House, History of Northern Nigeria Project 1973.

———. [Proposed Establishment] Arewa House, History of Northern Nigeria Project 1975.

History and Culture Bureau, P/069 vol. 1.

History and Culture Bureau, P/252, vol. 1.

History and Culture Bureau, SMG/AF/E/10, vol. 1, pp. 6, 51.

History and Culture Bureau, SMG/AF/E/10, vol. 1, for correspondences on the matter dated September 10, 1975, December 22, 1975, September 7, 1977, pp. 97, 122, 130, 133, and 137.

History and Culture Bureau, CO/E/10/, vol. 2, Archives Division General, pp. 411–12.

For a complete text of this decree, see *Kano State History and Culture Bureau Progress Report* (Kano: History and Culture Bureau, 1988), pp. 38–41; and A. Y. Hamza, Z. Y. Ado, Z. Gwadabe, and A. N. Shehu, *Taskira: A Research and Bibliographical Guide to Kano Studies* (Kano: History and Culture Bureau, 1996), pp. ix.

A THEMATIC EXPOSITION OF THE NUPE *AJAMI* MANUSCRIPT HERITAGE OF NORTHERN NIGERIA

Muhammad Umaru Ndagi
(University of Abuja, Abuja, Nigeria)
DOI: 10.5192/21540993020111

ABSTRACT

After the establishment of the Sokoto Caliphate in Nigeria early in the nineteenth century, various groups of Muslims adopted Ajami[1] *for transcribing their indigenous languages. The spread of Islam in Nupeland, like in other parts of the Muslim world, was thus accompanied by the growth of a local Islamic literature written in Arabic script. This essay calls attention to the Nupe* Ajami *manuscripts of northern Nigeria, with a view to clarifying their central themes. Previous studies reveal that the large intellectual output by the scholars of the Sokoto jihad includes not only Islamic religious sciences but also medicine, law, and administration. But researchers have not paid attention to the contents of Nupe* Ajami *manuscripts. I have chosen ten manuscripts for analysis in this essay. Seven of them are from the collection at the Northern History Research Scheme (NHRS), a postgraduate library in the department of history at Ahmadu Bello University, Zaria. The remaining three manuscripts are from collections in private hands. I have cited only a few lines from each, and have provided their English transliterations and trans-*

[1] "*Ajami,*" an Arabic word that literally stands for "non-Arab," is technically used to refer to all writings transcribed with Arabic letters or symbols in languages other than Arabic. Nupe *Ajami*, for instance, would therefore refer to writings in the Nupe language though transcribed in Arabic letters and symbols. *Ajami* was a popular medium of communication among Muslim communities of precolonial Nigeria, especially the northern region of the country, to which Nupeland was and remains an integral part.

Islamic Africa, VOL. 2, NO. 1, 2011. ISSN 2154-0993. www.islamicafricajournal.org

lations, followed by a concise commentary. By bringing this particular literary heritage to the attention of scholars, I hope this essay will stimulate research on Nupe Ajami *that could broaden our understanding of the Islamic intellectual traditions of northern Nigeria.*

Introduction

The state of *Ajami* manuscripts generally, including those in Nupe *Ajami*, is not quite different from the situation in which we find manuscripts in classical Arabic language today in Nigeria. These manuscripts, important and valuable as they are, have not been given enough attention by individuals and organizations in terms of their collection, preservation, and study. There is still insufficient knowledge of the actual number of these manuscripts, their authors, contents, and locations. Many manuscripts, and especially those in private hands, have remained susceptible over the years to natural disasters and damage in the course of readers' frequent interactions with the scripts. Agitations are ripe in some parts of Africa, south of the Sahara, calling for the labeling of *Ajami* works as "endangered scripts."

A major problem confronting *Ajami* works is the erroneous conception of those who link *Ajami* script to Islam, which unfortunately has continued to be abhorred by non-Muslim researchers, especially in Nigeria. The lack of standardized *Ajami* orthography is a very critical challenge facing students and even scholars of *Ajami* writings. The variations in *Ajami* spellings make it difficult, and sometimes impossible, for other than the authors of *Ajami* works to correctly read them. There are two forms of *Ajami* manuscripts in Nupeland today: Nupe *Ajami* and Hausa *Ajami* manuscripts, and both are authored by Nupe scholars. Since Hausa *Ajami* are relatively better known, this essay focuses on the Nupe *Ajami* that has not received any scholarly attention so far.

Historical Context

Nupe had been one of the languages written in Arabic script probably even before the influence of the Sokoto jihad extended to its land. It is evident that manuscripts in the Nupe language have existed since the fifteenth century (Ibrahim 1988, 98). In 1841, the Europeans in the expedition to Nupeland affirmed the ability of Nupe scholars to communicate in Nupe *Ajami* (Schon and Crowther 1942, 185). If the ability to read and write any given human language using Latin, Arabic, Chinese or other scripts defines literacy, the existence of Nupe *Ajami* scripts prior to the arrival of European missionaries and colonialists in Nupe country confirms that the nineteenth-century Nupe Muslim scholars were no less literate than the Europeans of the same historical period who transcribed their languages in Latin letters. Nupe poems written in Arabic letters indicate that Africa, to which Nupeland is a part, had its rightful place in the universal history of literacy.

By 1800, one of the few authenticated authors of the Nupe *Ajami* manuscripts preserved in the NHRS library, Shehu Abdurrahman Tsatsa[2] (d. 1829), had written Nupe poems on Islamic themes. Early and late scholars (including women) who composed poems in Nupe *Ajami* include Muhammad b. Muhammad Imam, Abdullahi b. Ibrahim (otherwise known as Man Shikafa), and Hajiya Fatima. Waziri Mamman Bida was another prominent literary figure who had more than 4,000 lines of poems to his credit, though in classical Arabic language. The initial collection and cataloguing of these Nupe *Ajami* manuscripts at the NHRS library benefited from the painstaking efforts of Professors John Hunwick and Murray Last. Their intellectual contributions to the analytical study of Islam and its literature and culture, particularly in northern Nigeria, cannot be ignored.

The wave of Nupe *Ajami* flourished in Nupeland as the most popular form of Islamic literary tradition among Nupe scholars until the end of the Second World War, when Latin letters through the introduction of Western education had already found acceptance among Nupe traditional rulers. Although not unexpected, the introduction of the Latin alphabet facilitated a gradual decline in the use of *Ajami* by Nupe scholars. Nupe *Ajami* was dislodged with the historic defeat of Sokoto jihad leaders by the British colonialists in 1903. In 1904 the Church Missionary Society established a school at Bida, a popular town in Nupe country, specifically for teaching Islamic scholars how to read and write the Nupe language with Latin letters (Fafunwa 1995; Ozigi and Ocho 1981).

---

[2] "*Tsatsa*" is a Nupe word that means "pure." The name "Tsatsa" was adopted for Shehu Abdurrahman from one of his poems, "Yagi Tsatsa," meaning "grandson of the pure." However, because of variations in the transcription of Nupe consonants using Arabic letters, which usually make such writings difficult to be read by others, this word "Tsatsa" has been transcribed in Latin letters by those who collected and catalogued manuscripts at the NHRS library, Ahmadu Bello University Zaria, as "Chacha." Authorities at the NHRS library have since been alerted to this transcription error with the hope that the English spelling of the word would be corrected accordingly.

The Nupe People

The Nupe people live in the northern part of Nigeria, within the north-central geopolitical zone of the country, otherwise called the "Middle Belt" region of Nigeria. The Nupe are found in three states of Nigeria: Niger, Kwara, and Kogi states. An estimated 85 percent of the Nupe population practices the religion of Islam. The remaining 15 percent is shared among Christians and atheists.

The story of the origin of the Nupe people goes back to one Tsoede, even though there are other legendary accounts of their ancestry. According to one account, the Nupe people are the descendants of one of the seven bastard children born by the concubine of the legendary founder of the seven states known as Hausa Bakwai (Eluwa 1988, 33). In another account, the Nupe people originated from Egypt. Other unconfirmed sources link Nupe origins to the Nuba tribe in the Sudan. However, the most popular of these views is that which centers on Tsoede. He was said to be the first king who assumed the title of *Etsu*[3] over the entire Nupe land (Nadel 1942). It was not until the sixteenth century that the Nupe became a kingdom. What existed hitherto were small Nupe villages under the chief of Nku. These villages were obliged to pay tribute of slaves to the "Atta Gara" who was then resident in Iddah, a town in the present Kogi State of Nigeria.[4]

Traditionally, the Nupe community is a brotherhood of extended family system, and polygamy is a common phenomenon. Every Nupe family averagely consists of members with extended family relationships including grandparents; great grandparents (however high); nephews; cousins; uncles; aunts; step-mothers; step-sons and daughters; and adopted children. Every native of Nupe sees himself as his brother's keeper. In conservative Nupe communities, a person's status is determined by the number of wives he keeps, not exceeding a maximum number of four for Muslims. Farming, particularly fish farming, is the predominant occupation in most Nupe communities in Nigeria.

Nupe as a Language

Unlike the Fulani whose language is Fulfulde, Nupe refers to both a people and the language they speak. According to Greenberg's classification, the

[3] *Etsu* is a chieftaincy title. It is used for the traditional overlord in a Nupe town.

[4] For a detailed account of the biography of Tsoede and his ascendance to power as the first *etsu Nupe,* see S. F. Nadel, *A Black Byzantium: The Kingdom of Nupe in Nigeria* (London: Oxford University Press, 1942).

Nupe language belongs to the "Niger-Congo, Kwa" language family, which consists of seven major languages (Stewart 1971). While some linguists argue that there are basically four dialects of Nupe language,[5] others, including Nadel, maintain that Nupe has twelve dialects (Nadel 1942, 19).[6]

Nupe is a tonal language, and has its own rhetorical system.[7] The Nupe people are very prudish in the use of their language, and their pedantic morality reveals itself in the euphemistic usage of terms. They distinguish between expressions that are suitable for polite conversation and others that are not. While the former usually take the form of euphemisms or circumlocutions, the latter, being direct, are considered fit only for "dirty" stories and jokes or for the more careless talk of young people (Nadel 1964, 264).

Selected Nupe Ajami Works and Their Authors

Abdurrahman Tsatsa

Shehu Abdurrahaman Tsatsa Abdurrahman b. Muhammad, popularly called Shehu Abdurrahman in Nupeland, is also known by other names, including As-Sharrif, Shehu, and Yagi-Tsatsa (Aboki 1991). He was born in AD 1756 at Gbaji, near Goba, a village located a few kilometers from Agaie town in the present Niger State of Nigeria. His father, Muhammad As-Sharrif, was said to be an itinerant Arab scholar who migrated all the way from Egypt to Nupeland (Aboki 1991, 86). His mother was the daughter[8] of the Imam of Gbaji village, where he resided for some time, preaching and teaching Islam. After the birth of Abdurrahman, his father finally returned to Egypt, leaving the child and its mother under the care of Abdurrahman's maternal grandfather.

Abdurrahman studied under various teachers beginning at Gbaji, where within a short period of time he memorized the Qurʾan, and later he studied at Etukpan and Agaie. He distinguished himself in many areas of Arabic and Islamic sciences, including *ilm al-balāghah, taṣawwuf, fiqh,* and *tafsīr.* He started preaching at the age of twenty-two. He toured most

[5] Namely, Basange, Dibo, Ebe, and Kupa.

[6] Namely, Ebe; Gbede or Gbedegi; Kusopa; Benu; Beni; Dibo or Zhitako; Kyadya or Kede; Ebagi; Bataci; Kupa; Cekpa; and Gwaba.

[7] A tonal language is one in which the meaning of a word depends on the rise or fall of accent. For instance, the Nupe word "*ebī*" could mean "knife," "kola nut," "pus," "feces," or "top of a hoe blade," depending on the position of the accent.

[8] Her name according to some sources was Aishatu. Others argue she was called Zainab.

parts of Nupeland preaching Islam with the use of Nupe *Ajami* Islamic poems. He went to such places as Zhima, Doko, Muregi, Tyabo, Dabban, Lokoja, Rabba, and Bida. He sometimes composed Nupe *Ajami* poems impromptu when the need arose. He was said to have instantly composed a poem challenging the request by the *swasun*[9] of Zhima village that he (Abdurrahman) should prostrate himself before him when Abdurrahman arrived there on one of his preaching trips (Aboki 1991).

Shehu Abdurrahman combined preaching, teaching, and writing as his basic preoccupations. His contributions to the spread of Islam in Nupeland included the building of mosques in some of the places he preached. He also introduced Islam to places such as Ekowuna ward of the present Agaie town, and Tyabo and Dabban villages, the last being where the mosque he built was named "*masalaci ti-kukurugi*" (short-headed mosque). The fame and followership gathered by Abdurrahman in Nupeland inspired him to engage in jihad of the sword against pagan settlements. At the advent of the jihad of Shehu Usman Dan Fodio in Sokoto, Abdurrahman decided to visit the former to study and take part in the jihad. It is claimed that Abdullahi Dan Fodio, to whom Usman Dan Fodio referred to as Abdurrahman, confessed that he had nothing new to teach the student who had come from Nupeland, given the depth of knowledge he had already mastered.

According to the earliest written accounts of Shehu Abdurrahman, the chief bodyguard and a soldier of Etsu Majiya[10] killed Shehu Abdurrahman at Kere[11] village in AD 1819 (1234 AH) or 1829 (1243 AH); according to some sources, while he was reciting the holy Qur'an. His murder could, perhaps, have resulted from the traditional envy and hostility which had always existed between traditional rulers and Islamic scholars in this part of the world. The Muslim scholars' call to the genuine service of Allah and their caution against evils and disobedience to divine laws have always earned them the hatred of those holding political power.

Shehu Abdurrahman was survived by five children: three males and two females. After his death, his children moved to Dabban where their father had lived; and from Dabban they moved to Bida, where the family house

[9] "*Swasun*" is the title of the traditional ruler of Zhima village.

[10] One of the twentieth-century Fulani rulers of the Bida Emirate whose grandparents took over political power in Nupe kingdom, which consequently led to the fall of the Tsoede dynasty.

[11] "Kere" is a village under Bida Emirate, about 36 kilometers from Zungeru in the present Niger State of Nigeria.

with a direct link to Shehu Abdurrahman can still be found today. Only three[12] out of many *Ajami* works of Shehu Abdurrahman have survived in manuscript form to this day. Two of these surviving manuscripts, "Eza Ga Yatun" and "Yagi Tsatsa," are discussed in this study.

"EZA GA YATUN" ("WHEN ONE BEGINS A WORK")

بسم اللّٰه الرحمان الرحيم

إزغايتن كايصوكو نيثنا   أثوغا شجو إتن ثغو
بسم اللّٰه ثويثم صوكو   أتنغى ياي د غميزو
طوكيامة

إغن ألولا تو نوف بتيممي   تو صلا كبا يمغوو يشتفا
قبلي تو بعدي مغتو ييى   مما غوزوا دغنغتو
الحقيقة

فرائض نيألولا غتوتو يو   يمغوو يشتفا
سن ألولا غتوتو يمو   مستحبو غو وثنيو
ثتوغة

Transliteration

Bismillahir Rahmanir Rahim

Eza ga yatun kaaye Soko nayitsu na
Acin-u gaa shidzo etun cige o
Bismillahi tsoici mi Soko
Atun ge yayi dagami yizhi o
To Qiyamati

Egan Aluola to nuwanfu be taymamay
To salla kebaa yimagawu-u yeshitukpa
Qabli to Baʾdi migatau yaye
Mimaga-u zowa degingata-o
Al-Haqiqati

[12] The three surviving Nupe *Ajami* manuscripts of Shehu Abdurrahman are "Yagi Tsatsa," "Tufya Tufya," and "Eza Ga Yatun."

Farila nya aluola gutota-u yo
Yimagawu-u yeshitukpa
Sunna aluola gutota-u yima-o
Mustahabiu guwo wucin yo
Ce tu gutaa

Translation

In the name of Allah, the most Beneficent the most Merciful

When one begins a work, the name of Allah, the Lord,
Should be put forward for the work to be good
In the name of Allah, my Lord Allah
Make good our work from here in this world
And in the Hereafter.

The issues of ablution, ritual bath and dry ablution
Including *ṣalat*, we shall hear it, let us listen
Qabli and *Baʾadi* I shall tell you
I can't exhaust it, little I shall tell
For certainty

Obligatory steps of ablution are eight
We shall hear it, let us listen
Superogatory steps of ablution are eight also
Its recommended steps are ten
And three (i.e. thirteen)

The manuscript of this poem is kept in the NHRS library of Ahmadu Bello University at Zaria in an envelope marked p.65/6. Another copy of the poem with little variations in transcription was obtained from Malam Musa Gana Daji in Jos.[13] This poem's title is drawn from the first verse, and it consists of fifty-four pentastichs. The first and second pentastichs introduce and enumerate the contents of the poem to include ablution, ritual bath, *tayammum, ṣalat*, and prostrations of forgetfulness (*sujūd al-sahwi*)

[13] He was an Islamic scholar of Nupe origin who settled in Jos, capital city of the present Plateau state of Nigeria. Although he died in 1990, it is claimed that he was born around 1880.

in prayer. As part of the introduction, the poet provides details on the number of obligatory, prophetic, and superogatory steps of each aspect of the Islamic worship *(ʿibādah)* mentioned above. The poem concludes with a eulogy for the Prophet Muhammad, giving the author's name in the fifty-fourth verse, the last line of the poem.

"YAGI TSATSA" ("GRANDSON OF THE PURE")

يا غي ثاثا ردو صوكو بى غنيم   يفا غادى توفى صوكو ثو عظيم
عبد الرحمان غباجثي إغي محمد   رى وغافر بى صوكو بى رحيم
إثو نكاج وج أث جين وغي صوكو   إثو ناغاياذ ثى دى نا إثو كريم
وج الجن طو ذج طو يكنغ   طو يشي طو يج طو فج طو كيم
صوكو رطاثي يربو يا وهاب   بو رسول محمد و غييم

Transliteration

Yagi tsatsa re do Soko, be gonimi
Yefa gade tsokpe Soko tsu Azimi
Abdurrahman gi Gbajici gi Muhammad
Rewa gafara be Soko e be Rahimi
Etsu naga jin wujin a ce jin na wun gayi Soko
Tsu na gaa ya zace de na tsu Karimi
Wujin Alijana zhi to zazhi to yakungi
To yeshi to yizhe to finzhi to Kiiʾmi
Soko Ryatwaci yire ba o yaa Wahabu
Bo Rasulu Muhammdu o wo goyimi

Translation

Grandson of the pure eulogizes God, I chant my poem
You (should) rely on God, Lord the Great
Abdurrahman indigene of Gbaji, son of Muhammad
I seek forgiveness of God, the Merciful
The Lord says: "Be!" and It is. He is the Lord
The Lord who gives for people to get, the Great Lord
He created the Heavens, mankind and animals,
(He created) the Night, the Earth
God the Beneficent, we ask you, O He that gives
For the sake of *Rasul* Muhammad, accept our prayer

The title of the poem, "Yagi Tsatsa," comes from the first verse. It is also called the "Mimmiyyah" poem of Shehu because it rhymes with the Arabic letter "*mim.*" The manuscript copy of this poem is kept at the library of the NHRS, Ahmadu Bello University, Zaria, in an envelope marked p.65/15. The poem, which was composed in verses of two hemistiches, consists of fifty lines. Aboki (1991) gives 1800 as the date of its composition. The poem is basically an admonition, in which the poet denounces forbidden acts including adultery, indecent dressing, and devouring the property of orphans. He also warns that hellfire is the abode of sinners as the punishment for their sins, while the righteous will be rewarded with eternal bliss in paradise. The poem concludes with a prayer upon the Prophet Muhammad (may Allah's peace and blessing be upon him).

Malam Mama

Alhassan b. Usman b. Ahmadu Zuruku is more popularly known by the name "Malam Mama," and a few of his surviving students refer to him as "Baba Man-Mama." He is also known as "Nma" in his family. He was born around 1890 in Bida. His grandfather, Ahmadu Zuruku, is said to have migrated from Sokoto via Kano to Nupeland around AD 1826 (1241 AH). He first settled at Raba, the then headquarters of Nupe, where he met Malam Dendo,[14] with whom he came to Bida around 1850 (1265 AH). Ahmadu Zuruku's house today is along Government College road in Bida, and is called "Emi Man-Zuruku."

Malam Mama completed his elementary Qurʾanic education at the same time with Muhammadu Bakudu (d. 1962),[15] who was later to become the ninth *etsu Nupe.* He later studied under various teachers including Liman Usman (d. 1935),[16] Alkali Alfa Ahmadu in the Banyuwa area of Bida, Alkali Alfa Yisa of the house of Imam Muhammad Shafiʾi in Bida, and Man Ndagi of the Efu-Nkoci area in Bida. The teacher who influenced him the most was Alkali Alfa Yisa. Malam visited many towns in Bida Emirate, including Gbade, Mambe, Dutsu, Boku, and Fokpo. In those

[14] He was the Fulani founder of Bida Emirate under the influence and authority of the Sokoto jihad leaders.

[15] This was at the traditional Qurʾanic school of "Emi Man Dzakwa" in Bida.

[16] He was the chief imam of Bida in the reign of Etsu Umaru Majigi (1873–1884).

places at various times, Malam Mama composed poems in Nupe *Ajami*. The circumstances that prompted him to compose his poems are alluded to in the lines of the respective poems.

The Nupe *Ajami* poet Malam Mama combined teaching, preaching, and writing as inseparable aspects of his career. Among his *Ajami* poems are “Egi na ma nya ba na”; “Etun na zai lo na”, and “Yekpe farila.” Malam Mama died in 1956.

“EGI NA MA NYA BA NA” (“THE ONE WHO COULD ASK”)

إغنا مينبانا اندمن تسا با نْيو　　مدا غنغبن منز أغن مفن غنيو
يكبى قبلي تو بعدي تسا غوسو　　مدا غنغبن منز زكوز تسا دونا
غابوبى غنغبنما غابوبى غنغبنما　　راتوا صوكو دى ديغيا غابوبى غنغبنما

Transliteration

Egi na ma nya ba na Ndaman tsa ba nya-o
Midaa gagbin manzhi agan mife gan yu
Yekpe Qabli to Baʾdi tsa gau sun-o
Midaa gagbin manzhi zakozhi tsa dau na
Gabo be gabgin ma Gabo be gabgin ma
Ryatwa Soko de degya Gabo be gabgin ma

Translation

The one who could ask, it was Ndaman who asked
I asked scholars they said I should tell him
Knowledge of *Qabli* and *Baʾdi* disturbed him
I asked scholars, honorable they are
Be tired not of asking, be tired not of asking
The gift of Allah has no limit, Be tired not of asking

The manuscripts of this poem can be found in envelopes marked p.65/4 and p.85/6. The thirty-four lines of this poem are focused on the prostration of amendment of *ṣalat* (i.e. *sujūd al-qablī* and *sujūd al- baʿdī*). Lines 25 to 29 are supplications as well as seeking for guidance from Allah; lines 30 to 33 are eulogies of the Prophet Muhammad.

"ETUN NA ZAI LO NA" ("THE WORK ONE DOES")

إتننا زيلونا ونغبنغنوو   إغ فوكبوز يفى غونمي
إغ فوكبوز غن أغبا تسويثي   إغابو بى غنغبنما يوا منز
زغوو دونا غاغبو صلا ما   كي أفى ملمي صلو غاني
لمن عي لا صوكو غن غوبا بى تنز   وغبوو صلا تسا صلو غاني
لمن فاسق جنثي غاغبو صلاما   كوغا فى مامي صلاو غاني

Transliteration

Etun na zailo na wun gbingan wo-o
Egi fokpo zhi yefe go nimi
Egi fokpo zhi gan a gba tsoici
Ega bo be gangbin ma ewa manzhi
Za guwo dona ga gbau salla ma
Kai afe malami salla-o gaa nyii
Liman gai la Soko gun guba be tunzhi
Wo ga gbau salla tsa-o sallau gaa nyii
Liman fasiki jinci ga gbau salla ma
Ka wun gaa fe Malami salla-o gaa nyii

Translation

It is the work one does that he inquires about
Fokpo people! Come and chant in chorus
Fokpo people have submitted to the Lord
Never be tired of learning, ask the learned
Here are ten people, pray not behind them
Be they learned, your prayer will be void
An Imam who associates partners to Allah
Praying behind him makes your prayer void
A dissolute Imam, pray not behind him
Be he learned, your prayer will be void

This poem has thirty-two lines, which are divided into two sections. The first section gives a list of individuals who are not qualified to lead congregational prayers, while the second section deals with actions that invalidate *ṣalāt*. Lines 1 to 3 introduce the poem, and lines 28 to 32 are salutations upon the Prophet Muhammad.

"YEKPE FARILA" ("KNOWLEDGE OF THE OBLIGATION")

يكبى فريضا ألولا واجب دونا	وكبى سونونوْ زيى بو فوم سنْبو
يكبى فريضا ألولا مديح دو تكبا	إبو غغبـثـزو مقيمز دونـا
فريضا ألـولا غتوابـا أتن يـو	غبانْيجنْ ووَكبويى أثن بو فوم سنْبو
نيلا بِي ينـيْ فريـضا دونـا	غبانْيجنْ ووكبويى أثن بو فوم سنْبو
نِنا غاأثغبن لو غواكبوا فريضا دونا	غبانْيجنْ ووكبويى أثن بو فوم سنْبو

Transliteration

Yekpe farila a lolaa wajibi da-o na
Wokpe sunoniu zhi ye bo fomi sun bo
Yekpe farila alolaa madihu da u tukpa
Ebo ga gbinci zhio muqimi zhi da-o na
Farila alolaa gutwaba atun ye-o
Gba nyadzun wo kpiu ye a cin ebo fomi sun bo
Niyanla be ye nae farila da-o na
Gba nyadzun wokpiu ye acin ebo fomi sun bo
Nina gwacigban lo gwakpa farila da-o na
Gba nyadzun wo kpiu ye acin ebo fomi sun bo

Translation

Knowing the obligatory acts of ablution is compulsory
To know its Sunna acts for the sake of the Hereafter
Obligatory acts of ablution, *Madihu* listen!
For the benefit of seekers, keepers of prayer
The obligatory acts of ablution are said to be seven
Strive to know them for the sake of the Hereafter
Intention and washing the face are obligatory
Stories you should strive to know for the sake of the Hereafter
Washing the hands up to the elbows is obligatory
Strive to know it for the sake of the Hereafter

The poem has eighty-nine lines. The date of the composition of the poem is unknown. The manuscript copy of the poem can be found at the library of the NHRS, Ahmadu Bello University, Zaria, in an envelope marked p.65/4. The central theme of the poem is on the basic acts of Islamic worship, namely *ṣalāt, zakāt, ṣawm,* and *ḥajj.*

Alhassan Zuruq Bida

This poet, also known as "Nmadoko," was born in Bida, but his date of birth could not be confirmed by his surviving grandchildren. Oral narrations indicate that he died in the reign of the *Etsu Nupe* Alhaji Muhammadu Ndayako (d. 1952).[17] His students included Malam Abdurrahman, Alhaji Baba Toko, Alhaji Baba Sonfadako, and Alhaji Baba Gbate. The poet is the author of a popular Nupe *Ajami* poem called "Yaji Ala Wojali." The manuscript copy of the poem used in his study is the one obtained from the house of the poet at Bida, in the handwriting of Adamu Alfa Umaru who hails from Gbacitagi village, near Bida.

"YAJI ALA WOJALI" ("WE RECITE ALA WOJALI")

بسم الله الرحمن الرحيم
ياجي ألا وجلي ياجي تو البرد
ياجي تو همزية إغو بى البرد
ياجي تو إشرنيا ياجي دواوي ما
ياجي تو وترية ياجي تو حيمعما
منفج أنيج أتو محمد يى
إثو ما دى أنيما يتو محمد يى
قطوف أزهار ما أتو محمد يى
وثو غزوزا وادى وحى محمد يى
محمد غأمنا أمين إغيمكثي
أيو رسول أيو أحمد مدينثي

Transliteration

Bismillah ir-Rahman ir-Rahim
Yaji ala wojali yaji to alburda
Yaji to hamzijah egau be alburda
Yaji to ishriniyya yaji dawawija ma
Yaji to witrijja yaji to haimi 'a ma
Man fa ji niya jin u tu Muhammadu ye
Yetso made aniya ma yetun Muhammadu ye
Kutufu azhari ma utu Muhammadu ye
Wotso ga zauza wade wa yi Muhammadu ye
Muhammadu egi-Amina, Aminu egi-makaci
Eyu Rasulu eyu Ahmadu Madinaci

[17] Alhaji Muhammadu Ndayako ruled in Bida as *etsu Nupe* between 1935 and 1952. It is assumed that the poet lived in the second half of the nineteenth century and the first third of the twentieth century.

Translation

In the name of Allah the Beneficent the Merciful
We recite *Ala Wojali,* we recite *al-Burda*
We recite *Hamziyya*, its subject is similar to *al-Burda*
We recite *Ishriniya*, we recite *Dawawiyya,* also
We recite *Witriyya*, we recite *Haimiʾa*, also
The scholar intends to mention Muhammad
You, too, intend to mention Muhammad
Kutuf Azhar also mentions Muhammad
If you too had searched, you would have found and mentioned Muhammad
Muhammad, son of Amina, Aminu of Makkan origin
He is called Rasulu, He is called Ahmadu, a Madinite

The poem of forty four lines centers on two thematic issues. In the first part, the poet eulogizes the Prophet Muhammad, emphasizing his unique and virtuous qualities. In the second part, the poet preaches against disobedience to Allah's laws and the need to avoid all forbidden acts such as backbiting, scandal-mongering, arrogance, adultery, abominable speeches, and negligence of the five daily prayers. In many lines of the second part, the poet keeps warning his audience not to combine litanies of the Tijaniyyah with acts of unrighteousness.

Unknown Author

The identity of this poet has remained unknown. Traditional Qurʾanic scholars and students in Bida and other Nupe towns within Nupeland could also not identify the author. The manuscript copy of this poem titled "Alhamdu Miji Yebo Ya Tsoici Soko" is kept at the NHRS library at Ahmadu Bello University, Zaria, in an envelope marked p.65/2.

"ALHAMDU MIJI YEBO YA TSOICI SOKO" ("I GIVE THANKS TO GOD")

الحمد مرجيبو ثيثنصكو إثنكاج أغج فلافلا
مرج الصلاة يمحمد غمكثي لبج بلى ذ مرج فلافلا
إثمربى إبى البركا غمكثي و ينبيلى يببى فلافلا
مدكى إني واجب بسنجي بمستحب بنبى فلافلا
يا يغمج يشتفا بونتلاشى تمث أغج أفني فلافلا

Transliteration

Alhamdu Miji yebo ya Tsoici Soko
Etsu na gajin a gau ji filla filla
Mire ji salaati ya Muhamadu gi Makaci
Labaji be ledzu mire jin filla filla
Etsu mire baa ebo albarkegi makaci
Wo yau bayele nya babo filla filla
Mibe ye koni Waajibi be Sunna zhi
Be Mustahabi bae ni bo filla filla
Yaa yegimizhi ye shitukpa ye woni tilashi
To mitso ugajin anfani filla filla

Translation

Praise be to Allah I give thanks to God
Who, when He decides, it is done clearly, clearly
I give salutations to Muhammad of Makka
With my capital I do that clearly, clearly
God, I ask Thee for the sake of the blessings of the indigene of Makkah
To give me foresight in this place (world) clearly, clearly
I chant the poem of the obligatory and of sunnah
And of recommended acts altogether clearly, clearly
O ye my brethren! Listen to the poem of Tilashi
And I too will benefit clearly, clearly

This poem consists of 110 lines in two hemistiches. Every line of the poem rhymes with the Nupe word "*filla filla.*" The poem, subdivided into twenty-five chapters (excluding the introduction), deals mainly with *tawhid*[18] and Islamic worship. The obligatory, prophetic, and recommended acts in respect of water ablution, dry ablution, ritual bath, the daily obligatory prayers (*salat*), poor rate (*zakat*), fasting (*sawm*), and pilgrimage (*hajj*) are each outlined in separate chapters of the poem. The poet also dedicates some chapters to explain women's menstruation. Like many Nupe *Ajami* poems, this one is difficult to read, mainly because of the inconsistencies in the poet's use of different Arabic letters for one Nupe consonant. The poem is also not dated,

[18] *Tauhid* is an Arabic word that literally and technically refers to the unity or oneness of God.

making it still more challenging to know the period in which it was composed.

Man Shikafa

His full name is Abdullahi b. Ibrahim Man Shikafa. He was born around AD 1800 (1214 AH). As a child, he was brought up at Gbara by his maternal uncle Nda-Adi who sent him to a Qur'anic school at Lade. There he completed the study of the Qur'an, after which he was again sent to study under Majigi, the eldest son of Malam Dendo. When the Tijaniyyah reached Nupeland around AD 1830 (1245 AH), Man Shikafa is said to have been the first to accept the new Sufi order. This most likely influenced him to compose poems on Sheikh Ahmad Tijani.[19] Man Shikafa, it is claimed, used to go in to religious seclusion for several days. Once, there was famine in Bida in the reign of *Etsu Nupe* Maliki (1884–95). When the prayers by scholars of his time failed to yield any rains, Man Shikafa at the instance of *Etsu Nupe* Maliki led the prayers for rain at the *Eid* praying ground. Thereafter, it rained heavily for fourteen continuous days. This event made Man Shikafa's students and companions ascribe sainthood to him (Aboki 1991).

Man Shikafa had seven children, four males and three females. The males included Ahmadu Waciko, who fought and died in the war against the Niger Royal Company in 1897. Other children were Ahmadu Rufai, Qasimu, Aliyu, Aishatu (otherwise called Nna-Mangegi), and Fatima Baya. The name of the third female could not be traced. Man Shikafa died around 1894. His literary works in Nupe *Ajami* include "Miya," "Eni Yebo Tijani," and "Laa Kaazibu." Here are excerpts from these three poems.

"MIYA" ("I BEGIN")

بسم الله الرحمن الرحيم

ميا مرجي يبويا ثونا جا ثجنا   صقو وش زنفى يا ذكا فوينا
جام جاتي كايى يثونا قبوثنا   الحمد يبوريجو ياثيث نجينا
أصلاة يشي بـي يا غي منا نجينا

[19] Sheikh Ahmad Tijani founded the Tijaniyyah Sufi brotherhood in AD 1782 (1196 AH). He was born in Ain Madi in the south of Algeria around 1737 (1150 AH). He completed the memorization of the holy Qur'an at the age of seven. He died in the city of Fez in Morocco in 1815 and was survived by two sons: Muhammad Al-Habib and Muhammad us-Sagir (Abu Nasr 1965).

صقو يـي تي وياي غوا طو بثي يرجيبو   ثوثي جبيري غطني نكن يبو
أبجي غيفى ذيتنوفى جيبو   أبوبكر غي أنس ثكوني رجيبو
يشي بـي غودوا يا ثيثي نجينا

صقوج أناباواج جيا غمكثي   ثيث ج ملائكوج جيا غمكثي
ثيث جف جنا طو نوا يا غمكثي   ثيث صقو يغبو محمد غمكثي
يشي بـي يرى يون ذكو نربينا

Transliteration

Bismillahir Rahmanir Rahim

Mire jin yebo nya tsu na jin yi na
Soko wacin a zankpe ya zana kpau ye na
Jama jati kaye tsu na yi kagboci na
Alhamdu yebo rejin o ya tsoici yi na jii na
Assalatu yeshi be yii yagi Amina nau mana

Soko yayi ti wo yayigwa to bici yire ji yebo
Soko ji yere gutwani fi nimi nakan yi bo
Aba Jiya gan wunkpe Zaire ta Nupe cire ji yebo
Abubakar gi anasi cire koni cire jin yebo
Yeshi be yii godewa ya tsoici na jii na

Soko jin Annabawa zhi jin ya gi Makaci
Tsoici jin malaiku zhi jin bo gi Makaci
Tsoici jin fe jinna to nuwan ya gi makaci
Tsoici Soko ya gba Muhammadu gi makaci
Yeshi be yii yire wun-o zako nare bai na

Translation

In the name of Allah the most Beneficent the most Merciful

I begin with gratitude to the Lord, our Creator
Allah is Exalted and Mighty for one that reflects
(He) causes laughter and cry, an attribute of The Powerful Lord
Thanks be to the Lord who created us

Prayers at night and in the day for the son of Amina
Allah created us with hands and legs; we thank Him

The Lord created nine openings in our body
Aba Jiya says he knows; giving thanks in Nupe language
Abubakar b. Anas composes the verse in gratitude
Day and night, we give thanks to the Lord, our Creator

Allah created the prophets for the sake of the Makkan child
The Lord created the Angels for the sake of the Makkan child
The Lord created air, fire and water for the sake of Makkan child
To the Lord Allah we submit; Muhammad the Makkan child
Day and night we call upon him, our beloved, the Great

The manuscripts of this poem can be found at the NHRS library at Ahmadu Bello University, Zaria, in an envelope marked p.65/5, even though the envelope does not bear the title of the poem. The poem "Miya,"[20] which takes its name from the first word of the poem, is a eulogy of the Prophet Muhammad. It consists of twenty-nine stanzas with five lines in each. The poem begins with the glorification of Allah in the first three stanzas and ends with supplications and salutations upon the prophet. No date of composition was given by the poet.

"ENI YEBO TIJANI" ("EULOGY OF TIJANI")

انيبو تجاني
بسم اللّٰه مركونبى سنا صقو   يشتكا يوو نيبو تجانـي
الرحمن اطيغنشي بى وو نيربوْ   ييبياني جنجن يبو تجاني
الرحمن طراتواثي وو نيربوْ   طيدان طريقا شيخ تجاني
اللّٰه طويثي صوكو بى وو نيربوْ   جنجن اصلاة غأمنا تجاني
لازن بى لوزن الو شيش يليلي   نم طريقا شيخ تجانـي

Transliteration

Bismillahi mire koni be suna Soko e
Yeshitukpa ye wo eni yebo Tijani
Arrahmanu Etsu Yegunci bewo nyi yire ba o
Yayi bayani jinjin yebo Tijani
Arrahmanu Etsu Ryatwaci bewo nyi yire ba o
Tsa dan Tariqa Shehu bo Tijani
Allahu Tsoici Tsu Soko bewo nyi yire ba o
Jinjin asalatu gya Amina Tijani

[20] "*Miya*" is a Nupe word that means "I begin."

Lazhi be lozun ala u shishi yeliyeli o
Nimi tariqa shehu bo Tijani

Translation

In the name of Allah, I start the poem in Allah's name
Listen to the verse in praise of Tijani
The Gracious lord of mercy, we beseech you
Grant us the foresight to praise Tijani
The Merciful Lord, the Bestower, we beseech you
Make us belong to the [Sufi] path of Tijani
Allah, the Lord, Allah, we beseech you
Salutations of peace upon Amina's son Tijani
This is fixed for morning and evening daily
In the Sufi path of Shehu Tijani

As the title implies, "Eni Yebo Tijani" is a eulogy for Sheikh Ahmad Tijani and the propagation of his Sufi order, the Tijaniyyah, with details explaining the rules and conditions for joining the order. The Tijaniyyah is very popular in Nupeland to the extent that even those who are not adherents of the Tijaniyyah seem to be conversant with its litanies and practices. The poet makes his knowledge and passion for Tijaniyyah very clear throughout the eighty lines of the poem.

"LAA KAAZIBU" ("IT IS NOT FALSE")

بسم اللّٰه مياني بسنا صقو اطو نني　　اطو يغنثي طأيبى بثنثي ولا غمغى بولوبولو
جوجو غنا مكايغنا مجير ادطا فى صوقو　　مجير ادتثا افاثى مصطفى لا كاذب
يغمز يغجن كودي يوما انيزو ثي　　موو يزى اغوغن كى اباينا يغمز لا كاذب
راي وابأبا نميزو يجي　　سن وغا بى كى نميزو بو لا كاذب
يغمي وثنأيب زالى وثيوو باتن　　لنيزلوغا بى ثنيا وو لى لا كاذب

Transliteration

Bismillahi miyaani be suna Soko Etsu nini
Tsu egunci tswa yi be bicincin wola gami ge bolobolo
Dzodzo ga na mi kayi gana mi jinri a de Tsu a fe Soko
Mi jinri a de tuci a fe Mustapha Laa Kaazibu
Yegi mizhi yiga jin kodayi nyizhema e nya zoci o

mawo yizhe a gogan ke aba yena yegimizhi Laa Kaazibu
Rayi wo a be baa nimi yizhe o yeji
Suna wuga be ke nimi yizhe bo Laa Kaazibu
Yegimi wo e cin aibi zale wa nya wo batan
La nya za lugwa be cin nya wole Laa Kaazibu

Translation

I begin in the name of Allah, the one lord
Lord, the Merciful; safeguard us from mistakes and make my speech
beautiful.
First, I acknowledge that there is no God save Allah
I bear witness Muhammad is His Messenger; it is not false.
My brother! Do not be covetous of this world; it will end
The comfort of this world will pass in the twinkling of an eye. It is not false.
Your life will cease from this world; and memory
Of the name is what may remain. It is not false.
My brother! You look for the faults of others forgetting yours
Leave others and look out for yours. It is not false.

"Laa kaazibu" is a sixty-five-line poem composed by Man Shikafa. The phrase "*Laa kaazibu*" is an Arabic expression that means "there is no falsehood in what is being said," and it is also the rhyme of the poem. It is a general admonition warning against accumulation of wealth and finding fault with others. Preaching the inevitability of death, the poem proclaims that drunkards, adulterers, and those who are not steadfast in prayers will be severely punished on the Day of Judgment.

Conclusion

It is apparent from the preceding commentary on each of the selected poems that the compulsory acts of worship in Islam[21] and the conditions for practicing the Tijaniyyah Sufi order dominated nineteenth-century Nupe *Ajami* poetry. For instance, the poems titled "Eza ga Yatun," "Egi na ma nya ba na," "Etu na zai lona," "Yekpe farilla," and "Alhamdu mijin yebo tsoici Soko" are all individually concerned with ablution and acts of worship including *salat, zakat, sawm,* and *hajj*. The Tijaniyyah Sufi order and the eulogy of the Prophet Muhammad are focused in the poems titled

[21] Namely, prayer (*salat*), poor rate (*zakat*), fasting (*sawm*), and pilgrimage (*hajj*).

"Eni yebo Tijani" and "Yaji ala wojali." Admonitions on apathy towards this phenomenal world, the inevitability of death, and the punishment awaiting sinners on the Day of Judgment are captured in "Laa kaazibu." The popular "Yagi Tsatsa" preaches against all forms of abominations and deviations from the righteous path. The central role of conservative religious themes in the literary productions of Nupe scholars could be attributed to the urgent need for basic religious knowledge in the early phase of the history of Islam in Nupeland when the poems were composed.

It is also evident from this study that the themes of classical Arabic literature of pre-Islamic Arabia, including satire, love, and elegy, found no expression in the Nupe *Ajami* poems of the nineteenth and twentieth centuries. The influence of conservative Islamic thought of the Fulani scholars, who laid the intellectual and political background for the establishment of the Sokoto Caliphate which consequently facilitated the spread of Islam in Nupeland, is another factor that worked against Nupe *Ajami* poets composing on nonreligious themes. Notably, nineteenth-century Nupe *Ajami* poets did not follow the example of the scholars of the Sokoto Caliphate who wrote on topics such as medicine, law, administration, economics, and so on. A frontier is left for researchers to penetrate and ascertain whether this absence of traditional themes is also true of the works authored by Nupe scholars in classical Arabic language.

Bibliography

Aboki, A. A. 1991. "Nupe Islamic Verses in *Ajami:* Edition, Transliteration and Translation of Islamic Studies Manuscripts in Nupe Land." M.Ed. thesis, Ahmadu Bello University, Zaria. 400 pp.

Eluwa, G. I. C., et al. 1988. *A History of Nigeria for Schools and Colleges.* Onitsha: Africana-fep. 305 pp.

Fafunwa, A. B. 1995. *History of Education in Nigeria.* Ibadan: NPS Educational. 349 pp.

Ibrahim, A. B. 1988. "Arabic Manuscripts in the Early Nupe dynasty." M.L.S. thesis, Ahmadu Bello University, Zaria.

Nadel, S. F. 1942. *A Black Byzantium: The Kingdom of Nupe in Nigeria.* London: Oxford University Press.

———. 1964. "Language and Morality Among the Nupe." In *Language in Culture and Society: A Reader in Linguistics and Anthropology,* edited by Dell Hymes, 264–66. New York: Harper and Row.

Ozigi, A., and Lawrence Ocho. 1981. *Education in Northern Nigeria.* London: George Allen and Unwin. 143pp.

Schon, R. J. F., and R. S. A. Crowther. 1942. *Journal of Expedition up the Niger in 1841.* London: Frank Cass.

Stewart, J. M. 1971. "Niger-Congo, Kwa." In *Current Trends in Linguistics,* edited by T. A. Sebeok, vol. 7. Paris: Mouton.

THE "NARZIGUAS," FORGOTTEN PROTAGONISTS OF SAHARAN HISTORY

Francisco Freire
(CRIA, Faculdade de Ciências Sociais e Humanas, Universidade Nova de Lisboa)
DOI: 10.5192/21540993020135

ABSTRACT

This article discusses the processes leading to an almost complete exclusion of some populations native to the western Sahara from oral tradition and historical writing. I will consider the Arabization of this context and its implications in the formation of contemporary identities, when evidence suggests precisely their complexity and non-linearity. In order to assess this argument I will look attentively at a mid-sixteenth-century letter sent to Lisbon from the Arguin castle, off the Saharan coast. This document should prove particularly important as the population depicted there as the main interlocutors of the Portuguese in the region—the "Narziguas"—is nowadays excluded from most historical accounts. The reading I propose of this letter explores the possibility of a Narziguas leadership in the coastal western Sahara prior to the seventeenth century; in this manner, questioning some of the well-established Arab-centered historiography and oral tradition. It is also argued that Islam has been ideologically and genealogically used as a privileged instrument in the reconfiguration of the region's social landscape.

Islamic Africa, VOL. 2, NO. 1, 2011. ISSN 2154-0993. www.islamicafricajournal.org

Introduction

In this article I will use a somewhat marginal mid-sixteenth-century document in an ambitious and provocative way.[1] By considering the privileged relationship between the Portuguese administration of the Arguin castle[2] and a Saharan population identified as the "Narziguas" (still recognized in southwestern Mauritania by the name "Nyarzīg"), I will challenge the hegemonic narratives that have defined most of the region's recent history. The evidence of this Euro-Saharan alliance allows me to discuss the possibility of a Narziguas leadership between Arguin and the Senegal River in the mid-sixteenth century, a period that is generally associated with the progressive settlement of Arab *qabīlas* (Ar., "tribes") and the subsequent decline of "non-Arab" groups (such as the Narziguas).[3] The prominence of an Arab-centered version of western Saharan history has been accompanied by a virtual silence on the role of the Nyarzīg. The importance of the "Rosales letter"[4] can be asserted in light of this almost complete exclusion

[1] This article draws mainly from the first chapter of my doctoral dissertation, "Narrativas *naçrānī-s* entre os *bidān* do sudoeste da Mauritânia: a viagem europeia e suas reconfigurações tribais," FCSH-Universidade Nova de Lisboa, April 2009 (funded by the Fundação para a Ciência e a Tecnologia: SFRH/BD/18668/2004 and SFRH/BPD/47681/2008). This discussion has greatly benefited from the comments and criticism of Yahya Ould al-Bara, Mohamed Ould Mawlud Ould Daddah, José da Silva Horta, Benjamin F. Soares, Sébastien Boulay, Maria Cardeira da Silva, and Abdel Wedoud Ould Cheikh, all of whom I wish to thank. I would also like to thank the interest and generous availability of the director of Torre do Tombo, Dr. Silvestre Lacerda. I am also grateful for the comments on a previous draft of this paper by two anonymous referees.

[2] Arguin—a small island of seven by three and a half kilometers, situated to the southeast of the present-day Mauritanian town of Nouadhibou—was first visited by the Portuguese in the mid-fifteenth century, and a castle was built during the following decade. The isle, and the castle, were then occupied by different European actors until the nineteenth century. During this period of more than four centuries the isle was used as a port of call for European commerce in West Africa, as it holds a permanent source of fresh water. For a comprehensive study of Arguin, see T. Monod, *L'ile d'Arguin (Mauritanie): Essai historique* (Lisbon: Centro de Estudos de Cartografia Antiga do Instituto de Investigação Científica e Tropical, 1983).

[3] The expression "non-Arab" refers, obviously, to the region's native populations and, generically, to a Berber ancestry. Still, this is not the operative term most frequently used in debating these populations, and the present utilization of the term "Berber" varies considerably from its strictly historical value, to the ideological purposes it presently encompasses in the southwestern Saharan region.

[4] "*Carta de Cristovão de Rosales dando parte ao Rei da rúina em que estava o Castelo de Arguim, motivo porque os castelhanos das Canárias iam ali resgatar a seu salvo,*

of the Narziguas from historical accounts and most oral traditions. According to most texts, if indeed any mention is made, the Nyarzīg are described as minor figures, losers to the Arab party that "conquered" the region. While some written and oral traditions can be found which declare the Nyarzīg as regional leaders in the past,[5] on the whole, they are considered as part of a non-Arab corpus, progressively subject to the southbound Arab *qabīlas* globally charted as the Banū Ḥassān.[6] I will use the Rosales letter in order to question this historiography and suggest a rather more important role for the Nyarzīg; a role which places them as political and military protagonists in the region by the mid-sixteenth century. But this letter also leaves us with an intriguing question: If the Narziguas were such influential agents during the first Euro-Saharan contacts, how did they so completely disappear from history? And, more importantly, who took their place as privileged historical agents?

The analysis of this document also allows us to question the processes which led up to the "stabilization" of Bīḍān identities in contemporary

---

pedindo ao dito senhor lhe mandasse um caravelão porque junto com outros que tinha intimidariam os castelhanos," Lisbon, Arquivo Nacional da Torre do Tombo (ANTT), *Corpo Cronológico,* parte I, mç. 82, no. 86, 1549. This letter was previously published by António Brásio (*Monumenta missionária africana: Africa Ocidental*, 6 vols. [Lisbon: Agência-Geral do Ultramar, 1963], 2: 398–400); Florinda Azinhaga ("A feitoria de Arguim e a expansão portuguesa," Tese de Licenciatura em História [Lisbon: Universidade de Lisboa, 1965], 238–40); and Avelino Teixeira da Mota ("Viagens espanholas das Canárias à Guiné no século XVI, segundo documentos dos arquivos portugueses," *III Coloquio de Historia Canario-Americana,* Las Palmas 1978 Conference Proceedings, 1980: 225). As with most of the *Corpo Cronológico* collection, this document is now available online at ttonline.dgarq.gov.pt.

[5] Freire, "Narrativas", 74–87; H. T. Norris, *Saharan Myth and Saga* (Oxford: Clarendon, 1972), 213; Y. Ould al-Bara, *La propriété foncière en Mauritanie: Dimensions sócio-politiques* (Rabat: Institut des Etudes Africaines de l'Université Mohamed V, 1999), 76; Ould Hamidoun, cited in H. T. Norris, *The Arab Conquest of the Western Sahara: Studies of the Historical Events, Religious Beliefs and Social Customs Which Made the Remotest Sahara a Part of the Arab World* (Harlow: Longman; Beirut: Librarie du Liban, 1986), 34; T. Whitcomb, "New Evidence on the Origins of the Kunta-II," *Bulletin of the School of Oriental and African Studies* 38 (1975): 411.

[6] The Banū Ḥassān are usually portrayed as a composite structure, associated with different groups of undisputed Arab origin that progressively "conquered" the western Sahara between the fifteenth and seventeenth centuries. On this subject, see H. T. Norris, *The Berbers in Arabic Literature* (Beirut: Librarie du Liban, 1982), 209; Norris, *The Arab Conquest;* H. T. Norris, "The Legacy of the Banu Hassan," *Maghreb Review* 2 (1977): 21–25; M. Ould Hamidoun, *Précis sur la Mauritanie* (Saint-Louis du Sénégal: IFAN, 1952), 39.

Mauritania.[7] The inclusion of the Narziguas as significant historical actors challenges the two meta-narratives which have hitherto been dominant in contextualizing the region's history: the Almoravid heroic achievements (which have marked an ancient and "noble" association with Islam, particularly through the patriarchs Abū Bakr and the Imam Al-Ḥaḍramī),[8] and the progressive settlement of the Banū Ḥassān (consolidated in the seventeenth century, and supporting to the present day many of the Bīḍān genealogical claims, based on a patrilineal descent from an Arabian eponym). The presence of the Almoravid and Banū Ḥassān *grands récits* have assured the exclusion of the Narziguas from most historical narratives by helping to provide, as they do, a coherent social framework.[9] This article illustrates a rather more complex landscape, bringing forth an emphasis on the "negotiated" character of the Arab *qabīlas'* incorporation into the southwestern Sahara.[10] In this sense, I will argue that the present social configurations portray an imperative affiliation with Islam, either at an eminently ideological level (via the Almoravids) or as a genealogical progression to the Arabian Peninsula (via the Banū Ḥassān). The western Saharan region might then become a legitimate Islamic territory, "purified" of the presence of any other heterodox actors—such as the Narziguas—generally disavowed of a clear Islamic affiliation.

It has been well established that Saharan history does not conform to a linear approach.[11] The region reveals profound social interactions, and

[7] Bīḍān: the Arabophone population of Mauritania, speakers of *Ḥassāniyya* (the lingua franca of all the western Sahara, with speakers in southern Morocco, western Algeria, Mali, Senegal, and Niger).

[8] R. Benhsain and J. Devisse, "Les Almoravides et l'Afrique Occidentale (XIe–XIIe Siècle)," *Arabica* 47, no. 1 (2000): 1–36; S. L. Burkhalter, "Listening for Silences in Almoravid History: Another Reading of 'The Conquest That Never Was,'" *History in Africa* 19 (1992): 103–31; P. F. de Moraes Farias, "The Almoravids: Some Questions Concerning the Character of the Movement During Its Periods of Closest Contact with the Western Sudan," *Bulletin de l'IFAN* 29 (1967): 794–878; A. Leriche, "L'Islam en Mauritanie," *Bulletin de l'IFAN* 11 (1949): 458–70; A. W. Ould Cheikh, *Eléments d'histoire de la Mauritanie* (Nouakchott: Centre Culturel Français Antoine de St. Exupéry, 1991), 11–22.

[9] Norris confirmed this same progression, using the vague expression "the descendants of the Almoravids" to fill the enormous chronological gap between the eleventh and the sixteenth centuries (*The Arab Conquest,* 44).

[10] My use of the expression "southwestern Sahara" coincides with present-day Mauritania's Atlantic coast, between the town of Nouadhibou in the north and the Senegal River in the south.

[11] T. Cleaveland, "Islam and the Construction of Social Identity in the Nineteenth-Century Sahara," *Journal of African History* 39 (1998): 365–88; P. F. de Moraes Farias, *Arabic Medieval*

to simply declare the submission of any of the parties involved in these debates is not a valid methodology, even if "oral chronologies"[12] tend to establish clear "cuts" in historicity: "Often, traditional accounts seem to be putting forward classificatory tables frozen in time, which all but exclude history."[13] Following this approach, rather than seeing the Rosales letter as a fragment of information about a nearly forgotten Saharan population, it will be used to illustrate a much wider point. It introduces the evidence of a multifaceted social history of actual contact between Europeans and local populations over a wide geography, linking the Senegal River valley in the south, to the town of Nouadhibou in the north.

This article conjugates bibliographic research with oral traditions collected throughout my anthropological fieldwork in Mauritania (several periods between 2003 and 2010). This combination of methods enabled me to better grasp the meaning of the Rosales letter, which, despite having been published, was never considered as an important element in the understanding of the region's social history.

The Rosales Letter

On April 10, 1549, Cristovão Valle de Rosales, the captain and "administrator" (*feitor*) of the Arguin castle and trading post (*feitoria*), wrote

---

Inscriptions from the Republic of Mali: Epigraphy, Chronicles and Songhay-Tuareg History (Oxford: Oxford University Press, 2003); E. A. McDougall, "Research in Saharan History," *Journal of African History* 39 (1998): 467–80; Norris, *The Arab Conquest.*

[12] G. Lydon, *On Trans-Saharan Trails: Islamic Laws, Trade Networks, and Cross-Cultural Exchange in Nineteenth-Century Western Africa* (Cambridge, UK: Cambridge University Press, 2009), 23.

[13] P. F. de Moraes Farias, "Pilgrimages to 'Pagan' Mecca in Mandenka Stories of Origin Reported from Mali and Guinea-Conakry," in *Discourse and Its Disguises: The Interpretation of African Oral Texts,* ed. Karin Barber and P. F. de Moraes Farias (Birmingham: University of Birmingham Press, 1989), 153. The seminal work of Professor Farias, even if geographically centered further to the east, is fundamental in widening the social and historical complexity of the western Saharan region, an idea he defended long ago: "Cooperation between nomadic and sedentary groups, Berbers and Sudanese, may have played a much greater role in the history of the Western Sudan than would be allowed for by the constantly reiterated stereotype of eternal opposition between them . . . Perhaps the time has come now for more careful investigation of the tendencies to complementarity that evidently also existed, and for a less simple (but more realistic) model of their relationship to be put forward" (P. F. de Moraes Farias, "Great States Revisited," *Journal of African History* 15 [1974]: 480).

a letter to the Portuguese king D. João III exposing his concern over piracy (*corso*) based in the Canary Islands (see Figure 1).[14] He informed the king that piracy was significantly disrupting the castle's trade, and he was also worried about their main interlocutors in the region, the Narziguas, themselves immediate victims of these attacks. Rosales requested that his king send naval reinforcements in order to secure an effective control of the coast, as the success of the Portuguese commercial activities in the region was suffering considerably from these "clandestine" operations. Rosales also informed the king that the leader of the Narziguas ("*senhor*

[14] Cristovão Valle de Rosales is not a well-known figure to Portuguese historiography, and was likely a simple knight (*cavaleiro*) of the royal house. He was vested the captain of Arguin in April 1543 by the king D. João III, having then waited to replace João Gomes da Costa as the latter finished his commission in the Saharan coast (Azinhaga, "A Feitoria," 175). The functions Rosales held in Arguin were to some point unusual, as it was more common in Portuguese commercial-military posts along the West African coast that two persons would take these different positions: a captain, dealing with military concerns, and a *feitor*, responsible for the commercial activities (R. Ricard, "Le commerce de Berbérie et l'organisation économique de l'Empire Portugais aux XVe et XVIe siècles," *Annales de l'Institut d'Etudes Orientales d'Alger II* [1936]: 266–90). The combination of these two functions might be due to the limited economic interest of Arguin (Azinhaga, "A Feitoria", 109; V. M. Godinho, *Os descobrimentos e a economia mundial,* 4 vols. [Lisbon: Presença, 1983–84 (1963–71), 1: 145–47; A. W. Lawrence, *Trade Castles and Forts of West Africa* [London: Jonathan Cape, 1963], 33; Monod, *L'ile d'Arguin,* 17, 21), but this hypothesis should be carefully considered. Recent research tends to attribute a more prominent role to Arguin—particularly during the first half of the sixteenth century—as an important port interconnected with a vast Atlantic network linking Lisbon and other Iberian ports with the Cape Verde, Madeira, and Azores archipelagos (A. de A. Mendes, "Esclavages et traites ibériques entre Méditerranée et Atlantique," Thèse de doctorat [Paris: École des Hautes Études en Sciences Sociales, 2007], 373, 409–12, 669). If, in fact, Arguin were a minor trading post when compared with Elmina (São Jorge da Mina), the activities developed on this shore should still have proven significant at the scale of the local economy. The continuous commercial activity of Arguin, the wide geographic scope that the castle encompassed, and its local impact, should suffice to restrain researchers from discounting Arguin as a significant location. Even if distant from an eminently historical reconstruction, this article might also prove helpful for the area studies centered on the European fortifications in West Africa: G. E. Brooks, *Landlords and Strangers: Ecology, Society, and Trade in Western Africa, 1000–1630* (Boulder, CO: Westview, 1993); G. E. Brooks, *Eurafricans in Western Africa: Commerce, Social Status, Gender, and Religious Observance from the Sixteenth to the Eighteenth Century* (Athens: Ohio University Press, 2003); C. DeCorse, *An Archeology of Elmina* (Washington, DC: Smithsonian Institution, 2001); R. Law, *Ouidah: The Social History of a West African Slaving "Port" (1727–1892)* (Athens: Ohio University Press, 2006); Lawrence, *Trade Castles;* A. Van Dantzig, *Forts and Castles of Ghana, Accra* (Accra: Sedco, 1980).

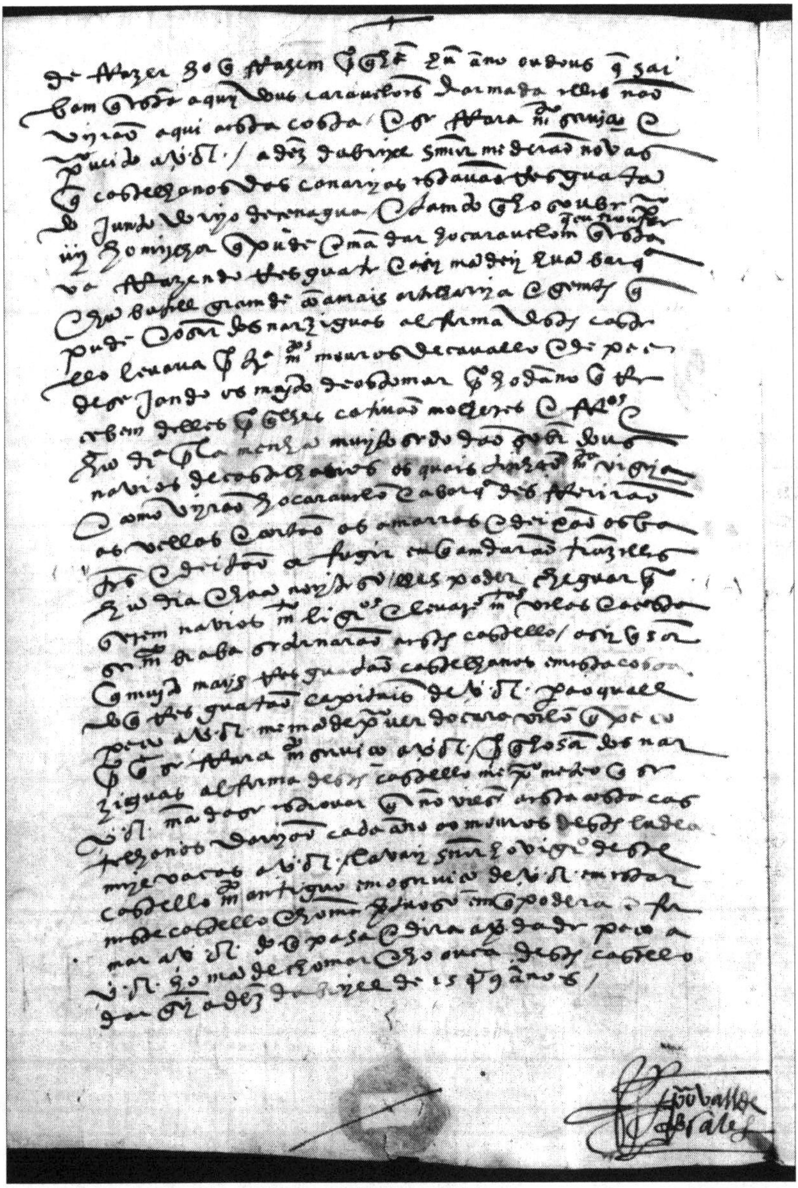

Figure 1

Carta de Cristovão de Rosales dando parte ao Rei da rúina em que estava o Castelo de Arguim, motivo porque os castelhanos das Canárias iam ali resgatar a seu salvo, pedindo ao dito senhor lhe mandasse um caravelão porque junto com outros que tinha intimidariam os castelhanos (1549)

dos narziguas") was willing to pay the Portuguese monarch one thousand cows each year for protection against the attacks perpetrated by "Castilians from the Canaries":

> On the tenth of April, my lord, I was given notice that Castilians from the Canaries were trading close to the Senegal River. As I found it out, I did the best I could and tried to send the *caravelão* I had brought here, but, as it was trading, I sent a *barca* and a big *batel* with all the artillery and people I could.[15] The leader [*senhor*] of the Narziguas, *alforma* of this castle, would take by land many moors on horse and on foot, hoping very much to take them [the Canarians] because of the harm they suffered from them, as they capture their women and children . . . And so my lord, much more trade is made on this shore by the Castilians than by the captains of your highness, and for that I ask your highness to send the *caravelão* I am asking for, and a lot more work will be done in your highness's name. The leader of the Narziguas, *alforma* of this castle,[16] promised me that if your highness stops the Castilians from coming to this shore, every year, they, the moors of this ludea, would give your highness a thousand cows.[17]

The three existing transcriptions of the Rosales letter are all in agreement, and are equally valid in an analysis of the original document.[18] Historiography has not, however, effectively used this letter nor the possibilities it presents for a reconsideration of southwestern Saharan social history. Teixeira da Mota, for example, one of the few who cites the document, substitutes the name Narziguas in his commentary for the generic term Moors ("*Mouros*"): ". . . the Moors, allied with the Portuguese, were victim of Castilian raids that took away their wives and sons and asked [the Portuguese] for naval support, promising to pay one

---

[15] *Caravelão* (Monod, *L'ile d'Arguin,* 48), *barca,* and *batel* are Portuguese names for the different kinds of ships used in the region.

[16] The expression *alforma,* fundamental in my argument, will be thoroughly addressed in the next section, entitled "Portuguese Arguin and Its *Alformas.*" The reading I propose of this term, as we will see, could translate as "interlocutors," or "allies."

[17] All the translations from the Portuguese are mine, except when stated otherwise. See note 4.

[18] See note 4.

thousand cows each year if defended against those attacks."[19] While this author's work is extremely significant, it remains important to point out that Teixeira da Mota's presentation of the Rosales letter is limited by its purely Iberian-centered analysis. The skewed focus of this reading cannot, however, be entirely placed at the door of such Eurocentric analyses; and one must also note that local narratives too rarely include the Narziguas.

Portuguese Arguin and Its **Alformas**

By focusing on the century when contacts between this region and Europe first intensified (1450–1550) we can provide some background to the Rosales letter. The Portuguese presence in Arguin dates from the 1440s,[20] and from the mid-fifteenth century to the mid-sixteenth century there was intense activity on these shores, with various European ships trying to establish a presence in a region which had hitherto been unknown to northern Mediterranean nations. Using the Canary Islands (but also the island of Madeira) as a logistical base, and working either for monarchies, through private entrepreneurship, or chartered companies, wealth was energetically sought in this region (see Figure 2).[21] The Portuguese monarchy was at this time the only European nation with an official presence on this coast, and trade lines soon began to join Lagos (in southern Portugal) and Lisbon (from 1463) with the western Sahara.[22] After an initial period of "conflicting intentions and practices,"[23] Arguin quickly became a pacified trading area for Portuguese authorities, with clearly identified local

[19] Teixeira da Mota, "Viagens," 225.

[20] Monod, *L'île d'Arguin,* 16–66.

[21] T. P. Grady, "Contact and Conquest in Africa and the Americas," in *The Atlantic World: 1450–2000,* ed. T. Falola and K. D. Roberts (Bloomington: Indiana University Press, 2008), 27–47.

[22] Documentation supporting the commercial contacts between Europe and the Atlantic Sahara is very scarce for this period, and most of the time doesn't acknowledge the local intermediaries in these transactions. The first known commercial contract recognizing southwestern Saharan and European agents only dates from the eighteenth century (T. P. Koltermann and U. Rebstock, "Les plus anciennes lettres des émirs du Trārza: Témoins de la politique maure d'alliances avec la Hollande et l'Angleterre (1721–1782)," *L'Ouest Saharien,* hors série 6 [2006]: 9–62).

[23] Brooks, *Landlords,* 124.

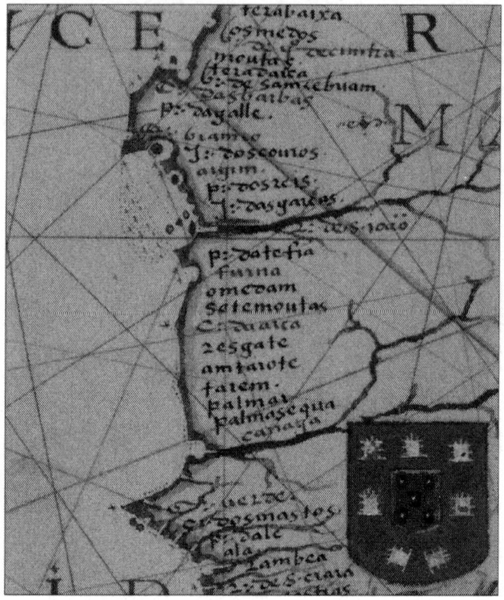

Figure 2
Atlas de Fernão Vaz Dourado (1571) (excerpt)
© Arquivo Nacional da Torre do Tombo

interlocutors supporting regular commercial trade.[24] Before exploring the Rosales letter and its significance in the history of the southwestern Sahara further, it is important to clarify the precise Portuguese use of the word *al-forma,* the expression which defines the relationship between the Arguin castle and the leader of the Narziguas.

---

[24] R. A. Austen, "Marginalization, Stagnation, and Growth: The Trans-Saharan Caravan Trade in the Era of European Expansion, 1500-1900," in *The Rise of Merchant Empires,* ed. J. D. Tracy (Cambridge: Cambridge University Press, 1990), 311–50; V. M. Godinho, *A expansão quatrocentista portuguesa* (Lisbon: Dom Quixote, 2008 [1962]), 329–35; J. da S. Horta and F. Freire, "L'arrivée des Portugais au cap Blanc et les enjeux de mémoire des premiers contacts luso-sahariens," in *Nouadhibou,* ed. B. Acloque (forthcoming); A. W. Ould Cheikh, "La caravane et la caravelle : Les deux âges du commerce à l'Ouest Saharien," *L'Ouest Saharien* 2 (1999): 29–70; A. C. d. C. M. Saunders, "The Depiction of Trade as War as a Reflection of Portuguese Ideology and Diplomatic Strategy in West Africa, 1444–1556," *Canadian Journal of History* 17 (1982): 219–34; G. Santana Pérez, "Arguin y Canarias durante la etapa moderna (siglos XV–XVIII)," in *Culturas del litoral,* ed. A. L. Bargados and J. Martínez Milán (Barcelona: Edicions Bellaterra, 2010), 45–65; J. Vogt, "The Lisbon Slave House and African Trade, 1486–1521," *Proceedings of the American Philosophical Society* 117 (1973): 1–16.

Alforma is a close rendering of the Arabic term *al-ḥurma,* meaning "honorability."[25] Cénival and Monod note the appropriation of this word in Portuguese during the fifteenth and sixteenth centuries, specifically referring to the local intermediaries of the Portuguese in North Africa: "*Prendre sous sa ḥorma signifie garantir sous sa responsabilité, sous son honneur. Les Portugais ont appliqué ce mot* [*alforma*] *aux notables musulmans qui leur servaient d'intermédiaires et de répondants dans leurs rapports avec la population indigene.*"[26] Another reading could also be considered for the word *alforma,* as the *Ḥassāniyya* (Mauritania's Arabic-based dialect) expression *ḥurma* also means a "protection tax" levied on tributary groups.[27] However, this possibility loses some appeal through a contextual analysis of the Rosales letter, but, most significantly, for the early Portuguese appropriation of the term further to the north of the African continent, when in contact with non-*Ḥassāniyya* speakers.[28]

Another letter from Arguin, dating from 1522, is particularly significant in understanding the effective use of the term *alforma.* This document, like Rosales's, refers to the problems created by pirate activity (based in the Canary Islands) on the Saharan littoral, but this time a certain "Bailelaa," who is identified as "an *alforma* of the castle . . . who has sometimes come aboard our boats," has taken "the ones from the Canaries" as hostages. In this letter the Portuguese official Francisco Luís Neto writes to Lisbon explaining the arduous negotiations he has initiated with this *alforma,* who was refusing to release the Europeans he had imprisoned. Although Bailelaa was on good terms with the Portuguese leadership of Arguin, for him it was a question of honor (*alformagem*) not to release the prisoners: "He had received *alformagem* that he would not return

[25] H. Wehr, *A Dictionary of Modern Written Arabic* (Beirut: Librairie du Liban, 1980), 171.

[26] Fernandes, *Description,* 158. See also J. A. F. Gracia, "Arabismos saharianos (Alforma, Alformaje, Alformar) en el español de Canarias," *Revista de Filología Española* 77 (1997): 149–52; J. P. Machado, *Influência arábica no vocabulário português,* 2 vols. (Lisbon: Álvaro Pinto, 1958–1961), 1: 198. The current definition of *ḥurma* in *Ḥassāniyya,* meaning "holiness," "*enceinte protégée, sacrée de la mosquée,*" is closer to standard Arabic: "sacredness, or sanctity" (C. Taine-Cheikh, *Dictionnaire Ḥassaniyya-français,* 7 vols. [Paris: Geuthner, 1989], 3: 401; Wehr, *Dictionary,* 171).

[27] P. Bonte, "Segmentarité et pouvoir chez les éleveurs nomades sahariens: Eléments d'une problématique," in *Pastoral Production and Society,* ed. Équipe écologie et anthropologie des sociétés pastorales (Paris: Maison des Sciences de l'Homme, 1979), 182; Norris, *The Arab Conquest,* 67; Ould Cheikh, *Élements,* 43; Taine-Cheikh, *Dictionnaire Ḥassaniyya,* 401–2.

[28] Freire, "Narrativas", 38–40; Machado, *Influência arábica,* 199.

them," Neto writes, "and among the Moors it was a great thing to break *alformagem*, [and if he does that] both Moors and Christians 'will not consider him serious'" ['*o terão em má conta*']."[29]

It is also worth mentioning a reference to a third *alforma*, useful in illustrating the vast commercial network already established in the region, and probably important for understanding one of the names attributed to Arguin. Presently, the island of Arguin is known as "Agadir," but in the recent past it was known as "Agadir Duma,"[30] a name hardly understandable today. While the name "Duma" is still used in the region, mainly as a feminine proper noun (common among the Awlād D'laim, Awlād Tidrarin, or Awlād Akshār), the origin of the Duma title remains uncertain, as no relevant personality with this name can be genealogically traced back to the mid-sixteenth century.[31] Surprisingly, however, another Portuguese letter from Arguin provides one important clue. This letter refers to a certain Duma as a "main *alforma*" ("*alforma principal*") of the Arguin castle: "these Jews are in the house of a main *alforma* of this castle named duma."[32] According to this overlooked document, Duma was a recognizable regional personality, and while genealogists have seemingly forgotten him as a memorable figure, he might well have been integral in the naming of "Agadir Duma."[33]

The interpretation I propose for the word *alforma* considers the Narziguas as "honorable" interlocutors of the Portuguese administrators of Arguin, who, after an initial belligerent period, established peaceful trade in the southwestern Sahara. The Narziguas were commercial and military partners included in the official policy of trade with Muslim populations supported in this region by different Portuguese monarchs. Through this reading, it is difficult to simply consider the Narziguas as part of the Portuguese regional clientele. The "allies" of the first Europeans trading in the

---

[29] Teixeira da Mota, "Viagens," 243 ("Carta de Francisco Luis Neto ao Conde de Castanheira," ANTT, *Colecção de S. Vicente*, livro 5, fls. 144–47 v, 1552).

[30] Monod, *L'ile d'Arguin*, 200–201; H. T. Norris, "Znaga Islam During the Seventeenth and Eighteenth Centuries," *Bulletin of the School of Oriental and African Studies* 32 (1969): 505.

[31] "*Que peut bien signifier le 'Douma' associé à Agadir?*" (Monod, *L'ile d'Arguin*, 200).

[32] "Carta de Pedro Valdez Rosales, governador do castelo de Arguim, expondo ao rei que, por falta de roupas, principal objecto daquele resgate, estava perdido o negócio daquele castelo de, que se aproveitavam os mercadores judeus trazendo-as de Tagos e fazendo o dito resgate" (ANTT, *Corpo Cronológico*, parte I, mç. 86, no. 126; reference code: PT-TT-CC/1/86/126). Also published by Azinhaga, "A Feitoria", 248.

[33] See also Mendes, "Esclavages," 449.

Atlantic Sahara could have been, at this time, rather prominent regional figures. This proposition, supported, as it is, by a single letter and disparate fragments of oral tradition, rests on a delicate foundation. Nevertheless, this idea has the heuristic merit of questioning the effective value of the expression "Arab conquest of the western Sahara." If the Narziguas were a recognizable regional force in the past, why have they been forgotten in most oral traditions and historical accounts? How influential was the European precolonial presence in the region,[34] and how significant was it for local history? Given this tempting evidence, one cannot avoid speculating about the coincidence in the chronologies which link the end of Arguin's "Portuguese period" (1638) and the disappearance of the Narziguas as regional protagonists. It is also worth pondering who became the privileged historical agents from the mid-sixteenth century onward. As we do this, let us turn to explore the exact contents of the Rosales letter, and the possibilities it encompasses for the comprehension of the precolonial social landscapes of the southwestern Sahara.

History and Syntax in the Rosales Letter

One of the most intriguing passages of the Rosales letter has to do with the suggestion of an annual payment of one thousand cows to the Portuguese king. This aspect is relevant for both the type of animal to which it refers, and for the very large number mentioned. How was it possible for an annual tribute to be made on such a scale, in a region not at all associated with large-scale bovine production?[35] And where did these animals actually come from? From the southwestern Sahara or from further south? But first, one must ask the question: who was actually responsible for paying this tribute?

---

[34] Brooks, *Eurafricans in Western Africa*; P. Mark, *"Portuguese" Style and Luso-African Identity: Precolonial Senegambia, Sixteenth–Nineteenth Centuries* (Bloomington: Indiana University Press, 2002).

[35] Leather (cowskin) was a fundamental item traded between Arguin and Europe in this period (Godinho, *A expansão,* 122–23; R. Mauny, *Tableau géographique de l'Ouest Africain au Moyen Âge d'après les sources écrites, la tradition et l'archéologie* [Dakar: IFAN, 1961], 380; Monod, *L'ile d'Arguin,* 17). Among other less significant items, the "modest prosperity" of Arguin during the first decades of the sixteenth century (Godinho, *Os descobrimentos,* 1: 147) was based on the exchange of wheat, horses, silver, and different kinds of textiles for slaves, gold dust (*tibr*), leathers, and gum arabic (Godinho, *A expansão*, 333; Godinho, *Os descobrimentos*, 1: 145–51).

The proposal to pay one thousand cows to the Portuguese monarch, in exchange for protection, is clearly made by the leader of the Narziguas ("*senhor dos narziguas*"), however, the responsibility for making this tribute seems to fall on the Ludea. Thus, it is reasonable to assume that by the mid-sixteenth century the Ludea were subject to the Narziguas, who were able to impose upon them a tribute which was to be made to the European leadership in Arguin.[36] The idea that the Narziguas were those responsible for the protection of this coast (following the Rosales description of their military intervention, "on horse and on foot," along the littoral south of the Arguin castle), even while supported by some oral traditions that endure in southwestern Mauritania, questions most of the descriptions provided for this region.[37]

The language and grammar of the Rosales letter, which are very clear throughout, pose problems of interpretation in its final sentence, which can be read in three different ways. The expression "*os mouros deste ludea*" can mean either: "the Moors of this Ludea"; "his [*senhor dos Narziguas*] Ludea Moors"; or "the Moors of this [land of] Ludea." These three readings lead to three contradictory conclusions: that the leader of the Narziguas was himself a Ludea; that the leader of the Narziguas "had" some Ludea Moors; or lastly, that the [Narziguas] Moors inhabited Ludea.

The problems raised by this passage stem from the "tributary" position presently associated with the Nyarzīg, making it almost unthinkable to suggest their preponderance over the Ludea by the mid-sixteenth century.[38]

[36] Another important thought for this debate was presented by Levtzion ("Merchants vs. Scholars and Clerics in West Africa: Differential and Complementary Roles," in *Rural and Urban Islam in West Africa*, ed. N. Levtzion and H. J. Fisher [Boulder, CO: Lynne Rienner, 1987], 21–38), stressing that European sources on West African history usually "focus on the central role of the merchants," when oral traditions, or Muslim chronicles, tend to propose other views (ibid., 36).

[37] James Webb, for example, portrays the "non-Arab" traders active in Euro-Saharan commerce as mere victims of Arab predatory raids: "Arab warrior groups continued to drift south into the Gibla [during the fifteenth and sixteenth centuries], traveling down the Atlantic littoral, perhaps partly in order to extort payments from the traders active at the Portuguese trading points along the coast" (*Desert Frontier: Ecological and Economic Change Along the Western Sahel (1600–1850)* [Madison: University of Wisconsin Press, 1995], 28).

[38] A period which most authors already see as clearly included in the "Arab conquest of the western Sahara": P. Marty, *Études sur l'Islam et les tribus Maures: Les Brakna* (Paris: Éditions Ernest Leroux, 1921), 5; P. Bonte, *L'émirat de l'Adrar: Histoire et anthropologie d'une société tribale du Sahara occidental* (Paris: EHESS, 1998), 228.

Nevertheless, a reading of this passage is still possible. If the present historiographic focus is kept, we could define the Ludea as a more or less clear genealogical corpus, but, in another common sixteenth-century Portuguese use of the word, Ludea seems to assume eminently a geographical meaning: the "*provincia de Lodea.*"[39] The famous text by Valentim Fernandes is particularly insightful in this regard. When in folio number 79 the author writes "the Arabs of this land of Lodea," he clearly states a distinction between a land, "Lodea," and its inhabitants, "the Arabs."[40] Indeed, there were Arabs living in "Lodea," but some non-Arab populations resided there too, like the famous *Bafur,* the *Azenegues,* or the *Zigüis*.[41]

Who Are the Narziguas, and the Ludea?

The Ludea are rather well known actors in western Saharan history, and are present in all post-Almoravid descriptions of the region. The expression "Ludea" is commonly used as a generic term, a "group name," or a broad social category describing diverse groups of Arab origin who settled in the western Sahara. Ould Cheikh, using early-sixteenth-century Portuguese documentation, identifies the Ludea with the "Wadāya," confirming, at that time, the Arab control of the north of present-day Mauritania.[42] Norris affirms that the Ludea are the "Ūday from the Awlād Ḥassān."[43] John Hunwick, confirming this genealogical progression, adds the participation of the "Ūdāya" in the trans-Saharan trade that had Arguin as one of its trading posts: "The Ūdāya were a branch of the Banū Ḥassān Arabs nomadising between Wādān and Walāta, and engaged in the gold trade from Jenne to Arguin on the Atlantic coast."[44]

The accepted version of the chronology and itineraries of the Arab *qabīlas* in western Sahara asserts that by the early sixteenth century the

[39] Fernandes, *Description,* 90.

[40] Ibid., 98. "Pacheco Pereira, who wrote between 1506 and 1508, is quite specific about who was then the master of the Mauritanian Adrār: 'All these nations are vassals of a nation of Arabs called Ludea'" (Norris, *The Arab Conquest,* 43).

[41] Those mentioned are the more notorious non-Ludea groups signaled in Portuguese documentation (see Fernandes, *Description,* 151–52).

[42] Ould Cheikh, *Élements,* 43.

[43] Norris, *The Arab Conquest,* 43.

[44] J. Hunwick, ed., *Timbuktu and the Songhay Empire: Al-Sa'di's Tarikh al-Sudan Down to 1613 and Other Contemporary Documents* (Leiden and Boston: Brill, 2003), 139.

Banū Ḥassān were widely established in the region and in control of its "commercial and strategic routes."[45] The information explicit in the Rosales letter, referring entirely to the western periphery of these routes, states, on the other hand, that the "*senhor dos Narziguas*" was a commercial and military preponderant figure at this time. When historiography turns to focus on the southwest of present-day Mauritania (where the Nyarzīg are still identified in oral traditions), Norris can only describe its "Arab conquest" as taking place during the seventeenth century, not referring to the Banū Ḥassān, nor the Ludea, but to the regional influence of the Awlād Rizg "Arab-Berber tribe":

> In the seventeenth century the Tashumsha and other Zwāya tribes in this region were protected by more powerful "Arab" and "Arab-Berber" tribes such as the Awlād Rizg . . . and after the battle of In Tītām in 1630 by the dominant Ḥassānī Banū Maghfar.[46]

As we will see more clearly when reflecting on the present representations of the Nyarzīg, this ethnically "corrupted" definition of the Awlād Rizg as an "Arab-Berber" *qabīla* is a fundamental element to take into account. The populations native to the western Sahara (like the Nyarzīg) experienced, from the eleventh century onwards, permanent contacts with Arab newcomers to the region, thus forming "Arab-Berber" *qabīlas.* And if by the mid-sixteenth century the Rosales letter differentiates between the Ludea and the Narziguas (with a Narziguas prominence in the littoral), it is very possible that the two populations might also have been closely connected. But first, let us consider what is known about the Narziguas.[47]

---

[45] Norris, *The Arab Conquest,* 44.

[46] Zwāya and Ḥassānī tribes epitomize Bīḍān "social order" (C. Stewart, *Islam and Social Order in Mauritania: A Case Study from the Nineteenth Century,* [Oxford: Clarendon, 1973]). The first, associated with religious practice and teaching; the second, with an "Arabic-speaking aristocracy" (Norris, *The Arab Conquest*, 246). The effective pertinence of these "classes" has been questioned, and this typology should now be apprehended particularly on its "versatility" (Norris, "The Legacy," 24).

[47] Surprisingly, the intensive ethnographic work carried out during the first half of the twentieth century by colonial experts (and military personnel) does not provide many elements about the Nyarzīg. Paul Marty's encyclopedic *L'émirat des Trarzas*, for example, only makes one reference to the "Oulād Nirzig," erroneously signaled as a phonetic deformation of "Oulād Rizg" (*L'émirat des Trarzas* [Paris: Éditions Ernest Leroux, 1919], 203).

Ould Hamidoun was the first modern author to include them in historical context:

> *Plusieurs anciennes tribus Berbères disparues ou presque, sont considérées comme Hassân, bien que leur origine soit antérieure à l'arrivée des guerriers arabes; telles sont, par exemple: . . . les Nierzig (Rosso), représentés par les petites fractions Taghrédiant et Idjegbadja.*[48]

> In the eighth and ninth centuries of the hijrah . . . , the Banū Ḥassān entered Mauritania. They swept away the rule of the Abdūkal in the Sahara and the Anbāṭ in Tagānit and the ʿAṣābah and the Īdayshalli in the Mauritanian Adrār and the In'irzīk in the southwest (al-Giblah).[49]

Three other authors, closely related with the work of this Mauritanian scholar, make brief references to the Nyarzīg. Norris affirms that the Nyarzīg are the descendants of the "ṣanhāja":[50] "The ĪdawʿĪsh, whose name some Moorish scholars [notably, Saddūm ould Njartu] fancifully regard as a corruption of Banu Wārith, one of the medieval Sanhāja 'drum-groups,' undoubtedly claim to be Sanhāja, and the term Anbāt is often used by them to prove it. This title was also used by the Nyarzīg of whom only a few fractions remain."[51] Ould al-Bara, following this perspective closely, associates the Nyarzīg with the Lanbāṭ, the leaders of the Gibla region (southwestern Mauritania) before the arrival of the Maghfar Arabs.[52] Thomas Whitcomb makes another short—but very significant—reference to the *Anyārzīg*, extending their presence to the Mauritanian Adrar town

[48] Ould Hamidoun, *Précis,* 46.

[49] Ould Hamidoun cited in Norris, *The Arab Conquest,* 34. See also T. Whitcomb, "New Evidence on the Origins of the Kunta-I," *Bulletin of the School of Oriental and African Studies* 38 (1975): 121–22.

[50] The ṣanhāja are "one of the principal divisions of the Berbers. The three major Saharan tribes prior to the entry of the Ma'qil Arabs into the Western Sahara were the Gudālah, the Lamtūnah and the Massūfah" (Norris, *The Arab Conquest,* 250).

[51] Norris, *Saharan Myth and Saga*, 213. The association between the Nyarzīg and the descendants of the Almoravids had been previously presented by the same Norris: "After his death [Abū Bakr b. ʿUmar al-Lamtūnī] the leadership passed to the offspring of his brother Yahyā b. ʿUmar. They bore the noble title of Anbāt. Among their descendants are the Anbāt al-Giblah ('Nyarzīg)" (H. T. Norris, "Sanhajah Scholars of Timbuctoo," *Bulletin of the School of Oriental and African Studies* 30 [1967]: 634).

[52] Ould al-Bara, *La propriété foncière,* 79.

of Wādān.[53] Following these suggestions, let us explore further the geographical contexts associated with this population.

Nyarzīg Geographies and Oral Tradition

The Nyarzīg have been persistently circumscribed to the southwest of present-day Mauritania, but, if we follow the Rosales letter, as well as oral tradition, it seems possible to extend this focus. Starting from an idea suggested by Théodore Monod, let us consider the geographical contexts associated with the Arguin Castle: "*Ce que l'on peut se demander, c'est comment s'explique le fait que c'est avec les émirs du Trarza, région plus méridionale, sahélienne et riche en gommiers, que vont négocier les autorités d'Arguin aux XVIIe et XVIIIe siècles.*"[54] The same Monod, in another work (*Description de la côte d'Afrique*), also speculates about the possibility of bovine production being extended much further to the north during the fifteenth century: "*Faut-it conclure . . . que l'emploi du boeuf porteur, aujourd'hui limité à la partie méridionale, sahélienne, de la Mauritanie, se pratiquait plus au Nord au XVe siècle?*"[55] This widening of the Arguin *zone d'influence* is interesting in dissipating a cultural and ecological divide between what is nowadays a clearly Saharan landscape and a Sahelian one.[56] If the possibility of extending the bovine belt further to the north of how it is presently recognized remains just a hypothesis, the mobility of the local populations and the regional amplitude of the trading activities developed around the Arguin castle might suffice to assert the surprising payment of one thousand cows to the Portuguese king.

---

[53] Whitcomb, "New Evidence II," 411.

[54] Monod, *L'ile d'Arguin,* 100–101.

[55] Fernandes, *Description,* 159. See also G. E. Brooks, "A Provisional Historical Schema for Western Africa Based on Seven Climate Periods (ca. 9000 B.C. to the 19th Century)," *Cahiers d'Études Africaines* 101/102 (1986): 43–62; Brooks, *Landlords,* 7–15; C. R. DeCorse, "Introduction," in *West Africa During the Atlantic Slave Trade: Archaeological Perspectives*, ed. C. R. DeCorse (London: Leicester University Press, 2001), 3–4.

[56] Webb, *Desert Frontier,* 3–26; J. L. Webb, "Ecology and Culture in West Africa," in *Themes in West Africa's History,* ed. E. K. Akyeampong (Athens: Ohio University Press, 2006), 44. See also B. Barry, *Le royaume du Waalo* (Paris: Karthala, 1985 [1972]); J. Boulègue, *Le Grand Jolof: XIII–XVIe siècle* (Paris: Karthala, 1987); Brooks, *Landlords,* 127; P. D. Curtin, "Jihad in West Africa: Early Phases and Inter-Relations in Mauritania and Senegal," *Journal of African History* 12 (1971): 11–24; J. F. Searing, *West African Slavery and Atlantic Commerce: The Senegal River Valley, 1700–1860* (Cambridge, UK: Cambridge University Press, 2003 [1993]).

The famous text of Alvise Da Mosto (or Cadamosto), who visited Arguin twice by the mid-fifteenth century,[57] could also be important in addressing these problems, particularly through his description of the region's social geographies. The Venetian author refers to the "confining" territories of "*Negros*," "*Azenegues*," and "*Alarves*," stressing the inter-cultural mobility of the *Azenegues* (among whom we should include the Narziguas): "[The *Azenegues*][58] live in some places of that shore, southwards of *Cabo Branco* and go through the desert, many of them to the interior, confining with the already mentioned Arabs of Ouadane. They also live on dates, barley and camel milk. But as they are closer to the first lands of the Blacks, they trade with each other."[59] This description, confirming the presence of the *Azenegues* in the regions to the south of the Senegal River, could finally relate Arguin to an area of intensive bovine production, and thus support the argument I surmised from the Rosales letter.

It is still accepted, in different southwestern Saharan social contexts, that the Nyarzīg "were the old inhabitants" of the region, and in some cases, its sole recognizable leaders before the establishment of the Trārza Emirate in the mid-seventeenth century.[60] In southwestern Mauritania, a small group of different *qabīlas* (the Taghrijant, or the Awlād Akshār) still claims a Nyarzīg genealogical attachment. Extending the presence of this population to the northwest, a "Nyarzīg cemetery" can be identified in the vicinities of Nouamghar (a village 400 kilometers to the north of the Senegal River) by the coastal Imraguen population, where the Nyarzīg are still referred to

[57] Godinho, *A expansão,* 368.

[58] "Azenegue" was one of the names attributed by the Portuguese to the Saharan ṣanhāja (see note 50).

[59] L. de Cadamosto, *Viagens de Luis de Cadamosto e de Pedro de Sintra,* ed. Damião Peres (Lisbon: Academia Portuguesa de História, 1948), 105.

[60] C. Hamès, "L'évolution des émirats maures sous l'effet du capitalisme marchand européen," in *Pastoral Production and Society,* ed. Équipe écologie et anthropologie des sociétés pastorales (Paris: Maison des Sciences de l'Homme, 1979), 375–98; Ould Cheikh, *Élements,* 68–91; Ould Cheikh, "Herders, Traders and Clerics: The Impact of Trade, Religion and Warfare on the Evolution of Moorish Society," in *Herders, Warriors and Traders: Pastoralism in Africa,* ed. J. Galaty and P. Bonte (Boulder, CO: Westview, 1991), 199–218; M. M. Ould Sa'ad, "Emirats et espace émiral maure: Le cas du Trarza aux XVIIIe–XIX siècles," *Revue du Monde Musulman et de la Méditerranée* 54 (1989): 53–82; R. Taylor, "L'émirat précolonial et l'histoire contemporaine en Mauritanie," *Annuaire de l'Afrique du Nord 1999* 38 (2002): 53–69.

as "the first inhabitants of the island of Tidra."[61] An adage recounting that "young Nyarzīg women [*azbat al-Nyarzīg*] drank camel milk and ate ashes" is particularly useful in an attempt to consolidate the geographical reach of this population; linking it, as it does, with camel production in the north, and with the consumption of cooked cereal in the south.[62]

Just as oral tradition continues to recognize an ancient presence of the Nyarzīg in most of present-day coastal Mauritania, Thomas Whitcomb extends this possibility to its northern limits. He asserts the presence of the "*Anyārzīg*" in the Mauritanian Adrar town of Wādān—another focus of the sixteenth-century Portuguese commercial efforts in the region[63]—associating them with one of its more famous inhabitants, the Idaw al-Ḥājj:

> It may be that Wādān was built or belonged to the *Anyārzīg* . . . which absorbed others and assumed the name Idaw al-Hājj in the ninth/fifteenth or tenth/sixteenth century, which would explain the disappearance of the *Anyārzīg*.[64]

This hardly confirmed genealogical exercise (unacceptable for the Idaw al-Ḥājj) raises an intriguing fact. The Idaw al-Ḥājj—still present in the town of Wādān, but demographically much more significant in Mauritania's east and southwest—claim primacy in the establishment of peaceful commercial activities with the Europeans, having initiated Euro-Saharan trade in gum arabic in the Senegal River margins, after having left the town of Wādān.[65]

These examples of recognizable Nyarzīg geographies are useful in pointing out the complexity of the social and historical contexts developed around Arguin. They assert that Arab presence is clearly not the only

---

[61] Another version of this tradition is still presented by the Taghrijant—the self-declared descendants of the Nyarzīg—who assert that the Ahl Nāṣr al-Dīn (a Taghrijant fraction [*fakhd*]) were the first to pasture their camels in the isles to the south of Nouadhibou (interview in Keur Macène with Sīdi al-Ḥamdi, March 2010).

[62] Professor Yahya Ould al-Bara is responsible for the identification and interpretation of this proverb (Nouakchott, January 2009).

[63] Godinho, *Os descobrimentos,* 1: 180–81; R. Mauny, "L'expédition marocaine d'Ouadane (Mauritanie) vers 1543–1544," *Bulletin de l'IFAN* 11 (1949): 129–40.

[64] Whitcomb, "New Evidence II," 411.

[65] Freire, "Narrativas", 164–65; Ould Hamidoun, *Précis,* 14–15; Norris, *Saharan Myth and Saga*, 214–15; Webb, *Desert Frontier,* 109–11.

pronounced element in western Saharan history, and manifestly not the only one to have left memorable traditions.

The "Corrupted" Awlād Rizg

When considering the Arab expansion processes in southwestern Sahara during the sixteenth century, one must closely consider the Awlād Rizg. In this region, as above-mentioned, oral traditions still recognize the Nyarzīg as its "old inhabitants" ("speakers of a language that was not Arabic") who, at a certain moment, shared their territory with the Awlād Rizg.[66] These references, supported by known chronologies and reinforced by the local representations sustained for the Awlād Rizg, might indicate that the expression "Ludea," mentioned by Rosales in 1549, could in fact refer to the Awlād Rizg.[67] Nowadays, it is the memory of the Awlād Rizg—much more than of the Ludea—which represents the prestigious Arab ancestry of many groups present in the region. The Awlād Rizg are described as "the first Arabs to have settled in southwestern Mauritania," and are sometimes depicted in close connection with the Nyarzīg. It is not my purpose here to explore all of these traditions,[68] but I would like to underscore that both Nyarzīg and Awlād Rizg are still recognized as groups that shared the territories now predominantly identified with southwestern Mauritania, prior to 1630/31.[69] In this sense, if we consider the Awlād Rizg as the "operative" Ludea "fraction" in this region by the mid-sixteenth century, the proximity between the Ludea and the Narziguas (as mentioned in the Rosales letter), is clearly more tangible.

Surprisingly, the foundational narrative presented by the Taghrijant *qabīla* (today settled in the town of Keur Macène, on the Mauritanian margin of the Senegal River) declares Nyarzīg and Rizg as brothers. This dual genealogical structure presents Nyarzīg as the oldest brother. Their

---

[66] Freire, "Narrativas", 67.

[67] The Awlād Rizg are, in fact, genealogically very close to the Ūday (Ludea) eponym: "Rizg ibn Ūday ibn Ḥassān ibn 'Aqil" (Norris, *The Arab Conquest,* frontispiece).

[68] Something I have attempted elsewhere (Freire, "Narrativas").

[69] "*Muhammad al-Yadāli, situe donc le début du déclin des Awlād Rizg, à la défaite qu'une de leur fraction—Liktāybāt—subit à In-Titām en 1040/1630*" (Ould Cheikh, *Élements,* 65; see also Al-Chennafi, in Norris, ibid., 63). For a description of the In-Titām battle, see A. Leriche and M. Ould Hamidoun, "Notes sur le Trârza: Essai de géographie historique", *Bulletin de l'IFAN* 10 (1948): 493.

Figure 3
Sīdi al-Ḥamdi, "*amīr*" of the Taghridjant, "heirs of the brave Nyarzīg" (Sīdi al-Ḥamdi, cited in Freire, "Narrativas," 86). (Keur Macène, November 2006). © F. Freire.

descendants fought many wars against each other, with the final victory of Nyarzīg resulting in the fragmentation of the Rizg fractions and their expulsion to the east.[70] This particularly engaging narrative has developed from the converging stories of two apparently opposed social agents (Arab and non-Arab), creating a conciliatory version of regional history. Still, it is important to note that if in most cases the presentation of its origins coincides with an Arabization process, the Taghrijant provide an inverse example. They declare Nyarzīg as their victorious patriarch and, to the present, their privileged ascendant (see Figure 3).[71] Following the Taghrijant genealogical narrative, one could argue that a clear divide between Nyarzīg and Ludea/Awlād Rizg did not exist; and, in light of this, recon-

[70] Freire, "Narrativas", 74–110. On the "dual foundation" model of Saharan *qabīlas,* see P. Bonte, "La constitution de l'Emirat de l'Adrar: Essai sur les formations politiques tribales," *Maghreb Review* 22 (1997): 40–54.

[71] One should also note that the Taghrijant reclaim an *ʿarab* status, thus clearly stating the difference between genealogical ascendancy and social status.

sider the proposal of an annual tribute of one thousand cows made by the leader of the Narziguas to the Portuguese authorities in Arguin.

How is it conceivable to associate the Awlād Rizg (a genealogically Arab group, associated with the Ludea) and large-scale bovine production? The *qabīlas* of Arab origin—and fundamentally, of *ʿarab* status—are mainly characterized by their lack of "productivity," their predatory raids and vast camel routes, but never with cattle-rearing or the maintenance of the wells required for large-scale cattle production.[72] In fact, the descriptions pertaining to the Awlād Rizg have little to do with this caricature. Oral tradition describes the construction of close and fruitful ties between the Awlād Rizg and the local populations, to the extent that they are sometimes taken as an example of "promiscuous" relations between Arabs and non-Arabs.[73] The Awlād Rizg, as they were described to me in southwestern Mauritania, are most notably said to have been owners of wells, cattle, and pasture grounds. This "constructive" reading of the Awlād Rizg suggests that one should carefully consider the Arab "conquest" of the western Sahara, and the image that persistently portrays Arab *qabīlas* as intensively nomadic, exclusively associated with camel-herding, with no ownership of land, and dependent on tributes extracted from frightened populations.[74] In fact, this image is not consistent with my reading of the

[72] "*Comme tous les Arabes, les Maures font une distinction entre les 'beggâra,' gents des boeufs, et les 'ebbâla,' éleveurs de chameaux; et ils disent: 'El 'ibel mâhi moulk ez-zâwî; ellî moulk ez-zâwî lebger = les chameaux ne sont pas le bien du marabout; ce qui est le bien du marabout, c'est les bovidés'*" (Leriche and Ould Hamidoun, "Notes," 526).

[73] This idea is epitomized in the declared possibility of the Awlād Rizg having lost their original Arabic language for the *klām aznāga* (the Berber dialect of the southwestern Sahara). On this question, see also M. Al-Chennafi, "How the *Ḥassāniyya* Vernacular of Mauritania Supplanted Zenaga," *Maghreb Review* 6 (1981): 77–78; P. Bonte, "Guerriers et repentants: Les *tawba* et l'évolution politique de la société émirale maure," *Al Wasît: Bulletin du Institut Mauritanien de Recherche Scientifique* 3 (1989): 5–18; Bonte, *L'émirat de l'Adrar,* 231; P. Dubié, "L'îlot berbérophone de Mauritanie," *Bulletin de l'IFAN* 2 (1940): 316–25; Freire, "Narrativas", 67; B. S. Hall, "The Question of 'Race' in the Pre-Colonial Southern Sahara," *Journal of North African Studies* 10, nos. 3–4 (2005): 339–67; Norris, *The Arab Conquest,* xx–ii; Norris, "The Legacy," 24; Ould Cheikh, *Élements,* 71–72; C. Taine-Cheikh, "Les langues comme enjeux identitaires," *Politique Africaine* 55 (1994): 57–65; C. Taine-Cheikh, *Dictionnaire zénaga-français* (Cologne: Rüdiger Köppe Verlag, 2008); R. Taylor, "Warriors, Tributaries, Blood Money and Political Transformation in Nineteenth-Century Mauritania," *Journal of African History* 36 (1995): 419–41; Webb, *Desert Frontier,* 28.

[74] An idea generally linked to the consolidation of the Banū Maghfar political influence in the southwestern Sahara. This group, included in the Ḥassān "extended family," is associated with the centralization of political administration in the Trārza and Brākna regions of

above-cited sources.[75] The fact that the Awlād Rizg might have been associated with cattle-rearing gives us an unequivocal example of this, thus also proving the complexity of the social constructs in this region at a defining moment in its history.

Conclusion

This article highlights the need for an integrated and flexible reading of western Saharan history. By "disrupting" the dominant conceptions of the region's history, it asserts that a rather more complex social pattern existed during the mid-sixteenth century.[76] This is a key moment when there is increased contact with European traders, and a consolidation of Arab political and cultural influence. It is also a period in which written sources on the region are scarce, and for this reason the Rosales letter is a significant source. The most notable aspect of this letter is, however, the identification of the Narziguas as interlocutors of the Portuguese authorities present in Arguin at this time. Contrary to the well-established historical tradition, the Rosales letter emphasizes the role of the Narziguas: the privileged interlocutors of the Portuguese, the leaders of the fight against "the Castilians from the Canaries." This evidence allows us to openly question the exclusion of the Narziguas/Nyarzīg as influential agents in the region's history.

Furthermore, the material presented here points to the intensity of the precolonial Euro-Saharan encounters. Today, the most visible narratives of identity, formed after debates now centuries old (focusing mainly on the Mauritanian Bīḍān population), are those showing a clear degree of proximity with the Arabic Peninsula at the time of the Prophet. As such, the participation of the Narziguas (a population disavowed of a credible Islamic genealogical project) in early Euro-Saharan contacts, and

---

present-day Mauritania, from the mid-seventeenth century to the colonial period. See Ould Saʿad, "Emirats."

[75] Writing in the early twentieth century, P. Marty helped to consolidate this stereotype: "*les coutumes arabes, négatives ou oppressives, issues d'un nomadisme invétéré, impropre à toute évolution sérieuse*" (Marty, *Études sur l'Islam,* 8).

[76] As already signaled by different authors: Bonte, *L'émirat de l'Adrar*; T. Cleaveland, *Becoming Walata: A History of Saharan Social Formation and Transformation* (Portsmouth: Heinemann, 2002); P. F. de Moraes Farias, "Silent Trade: Myth and Historical Evidence," *History in Africa* 1 (1974): 9–24; Lydon, *On Trans-Saharan Trails;* Searing, *West African Slavery;* Norris, *The Arab Conquest;* Taylor, "L'émirat précolonial"; Whitcomb, "New Evidence I"; Whitcomb, "New Evidence II."

their prevailing responsibility for the protection of a vast littoral region, should not be considered historically important. The now-legitimate interpreters of historical narratives have an interest in presenting genealogical structures that connect to the cradle of Islam, denying any reference to non-Arab participants in the region's long-term historical processes. Accordingly, there has been a progressive "downgrading" of the role which such populations played as historical agents; the Nyarzīg participation in the Atlantic trade, for example, remains concealed and largely unexplored.

The denial of a determinant role for the Narziguas also materializes a deliberate effort to support Islamic legitimacy for the region's populations. As mentioned above, the predominant narratives in regional history utilize primarily either the Almoravid epic, or the Banū Ḥassān seventeenth-century "conquest" of the southwestern Sahara, in order to legitimate Islamic credentials. The implausibility of the Arab genealogies of most of the participants in the Almoravid movement, and the "recent" settlement of the Banū Ḥassān in the region, are not enough evidence to discharge these actors from guaranteeing a "noble" Islamic ascendancy. These processes of accentuated genealogical "normalization" contribute to the incorporation of a linear Arab/Islamic ancestry in a now-"purified" region, where any heterodox forms of affiliation (not directly associated with the Arabian Peninsula and the Prophetic lineages) are disregarded. The need for an effective Islamic affiliation could then explain the exclusion of the Nyarzīg as significant contributors to the region's history, and justify the emergence of other protagonists.

Bibliography

Al-Chennafi, M. Mohammed. "How the *Ḥassāniyya* Vernacular of Mauritania Supplanted Zenaga." *Maghreb Review* 6 (1981): 77–78.

Austen, Ralph A. "Marginalization, Stagnation, and Growth: The Trans-Saharan Caravan Trade in the Era of European Expansion, 1500–1900." In *The Rise of Merchant Empires,* ed. J. D. Tracy. Cambridge, UK: Cambridge University Press, 1990, 311–50.

Azinhaga, Florinda. "A feitoria de Arguim e a expansão portuguesa." Tese de Licenciatura em História. Lisbon: Universidade de Lisboa, 1965.

Barry, Bubacar. *Le royaume du Waalo*. Paris: Karthala, 1985 (1972).

Benhsain, R., and Jean Devisse. "Les Almoravides et l'Afrique Occidentale (XIe–XIIe Siècle)." *Arabica* 47, no. 1 (2000): 1–36.

Bonte, Pierre. "Segmentarité et pouvoir chez les éleveurs nomades sahariens: Eléments d'une problématique." In *Pastoral Production and Society,* ed. Équipe écologie et anthropologie des sociétés pastorals. Paris: Maison des Sciences de l'Homme, 1979, 171–200.

———. "Guerriers et repentants: Les *tawba* et l'évolution politique de la société émirale maure." *Al Wasît: Bulletin du Institut Mauritanien de Recherche Scientifique* 3 (1989): 5–18.

———. "La constitution de l'Emirat de l'Adrar: Essai sur les formations politiques tribales." *Maghreb Review* 22 (1997): 40–54.

———. "L'émirat de l'Adrar. Histoire et anthropologie d'une société tribale du Sahara occidental." Thèse d'État. Paris: École des Hautes Études en Sciences Sociales , 1998.

Boulègue, Jean. *Le Grand Jolof: XIII–XVIe siècle.* Paris: Karthala, 1987.

Brásio, António, ed. *Monumenta Missionaria Africana, África Ocidental (1500–1569)*, 6 vols. Lisbon: Agência-Geral do Ultramar and Academia Portuguesa de História, 1958–1991.

Brooks, George E. "A Provisional Historical Schema for Western Africa Based on Seven Climate Periods (ca. 9000 B.C. to the 19th Century)." *Cahiers d'Études Africaines* 101/102 (1986): 43–62.

———. *Landlords and Strangers: Ecology, Society, and Trade in Western Africa, 1000-1630.* Boulder, CO: Westview, 1993.

———. *Eurafricans in Western Africa: Commerce, Social Status, Gender, and Religious Observance from the Sixteenth to the Eighteenth Century.* Athens: Ohio University Press, 2003.

Burkhalter, Sheryl L. "Listening for Silences in Almoravid History: Another Reading of 'the Conquest That Never Was.'" *History in Africa* 19 (1992): 103–31.

Cadamosto, Luis de. *Viagens de Luis de Cadamosto e de Pedro de Sintra.* Edited by Damião Peres. Lisbon: Academia Portuguesa de História, 1948.

Cleaveland, Timothy. "Islam and the Construction of Social Identity in the Nineteenth-Century Sahara." *Journal of African History* 39 (1998): 365–88.

———. *Becoming Walata: A History of Saharan Social Formation and Transformation.* Portsmouth: Heinemann, 2002.

Curtin, Philip D. "Jihad in West Africa: Early Phases and Inter-Relations in Mauritania and Senegal." *Journal of African History* 12 (1971): 11–24.

De Moraes Farias, Paulo Fernando. "The Almoravids: Some Questions Concerning the Character of the Movement During Its Periods of Closest Contact with the Western Sudan." *Bulletin de l'IFAN* 29 (1967): 794–878.

———. “Great States Revisited.” *Journal of African History* 15 (1974): 479–88.

———. “Silent Trade: Myth and Historical Evidence.” *History in Africa* 1 (1974): 9–24.

———. “Pilgrimages to ‘Pagan’ Mecca in Mandenka Stories of Origin Reported from Mali and Guinea-Conakry.” In *Discourse and Its Disguises: The Interpretation of African Oral Texts,* ed. Karin Barber and P. F. de Moraes Farias. Birmingham: University of Birmingham, 1989, 152–70.

———. *Arabic Medieval Inscriptions from the Republic of Mali: Epigraphy, Chronicles and Songhay-Tuareg History.* Oxford: Oxford University Press, 2003.

DeCorse, Christopher R. *An Archeology of Elmina.* Washington, DC: Smithsonian Institution, 2001.

———. “Introduction.” In *West Africa During the Atlantic Slave Trade: Archaeological Perspectives,* ed. Christopher R. DeCorse. London: Leicester University Press, 2001, 1–13.

Dubié, Paul. “L’îlot berbérophone de Mauritanie.” *Bulletin de l’IFAN* 2 (1940): 316–25.

Fernandes, Valentim. *Description de la côte d’Afrique de Ceuta au Sénégal par Valentim Fernandes (1506–1507)*. Edited by Pierre de Cénival and Théodore Monod. Paris: Comité d’État Historique et Scientifique de l’A.O.F., 1938.

Freire, Francisco. “Narrativas *naçrānī-s* entre os *bidān* do sudoeste da Mauritânia: A viagem europeia e suas reconfigurações tribais.” Tese de Doutoramento. Lisbon: FCSH-Universidade Nova de Lisboa, 2009.

Godinho, V. M. *Os descobrimentos e a economia mundial.* 4 vols. Lisbon: Presença, 1983–84 (1963–71).

———. *A expansão quatrocentista portuguesa.* Lisbon: Dom Quixote, 2008 (1962).

Gracia, J. A. F. “Arabismos saharianos (Alforma, Alformaje, Alformar) en el español de Canarias.” *Revista de Filología Española* 77 (1997): 149–52.

Grady, Timothy P. “Contact and Conquest in Africa and the Americas.” In *The Atlantic World: 1450–2000,* ed. Toyin Falola and Kevin David Roberts. Bloomington: Indiana University Press, 2008, 27–47.

Hall, Bruce S. “The Question of ‘Race’ in the Pre-Colonial Southern Sahara.” *Journal of North African Studies* 10, nos. 3–4 (2005): 339–67.

Hamès, Constant. “L’évolution des émirats maures sous l’effet du capitalisme marchand européen.” In *Pastoral Production and Society,* ed. Équipe écologie et anthropologie des sociétés pastorals. Paris: Maison des Sciences de l’Homme, 1979, 375–98.

Horta, José da Silva, and Francisco Freire. "L'arrivée des Portugais au cap Blanc et les enjeux de mémoire des premiers contacts luso-sahariens." In *Nouadhibou: Fortunes et infortunes de la 'capitale économique' mauritanienne,* ed. Benjamin Acloque. Forthcoming.

Hunwick, John, ed. *Timbuktu and the Songhay Empire: Al-Sa'di's Tarikh al-Sudan down to 1613 and Other Contemporary Documents.* Leiden and Boston: Brill, 2003 (1998).

Koltermann, T. P., and Ulrich Rebstock. "Les plus anciennes lettres des émirs du Trarza: Témoins de la politique maure d'alliances avec la Hollande et l'Angleterre (1721–1782)." *L'Ouest Saharien,* hors série 6 (2006): 9–62.

Law, Robin. *Ouidah: The Social History of a West African Slaving 'Port' (1727–1892).* Athens: Ohio University Press, 2006 (2004).

Lawrence, A. W. *Trade Castles and Forts of West Africa.* London: Jonathan Cape, 1963.

Leriche, Albert. "L'Islam en Mauritanie." *Bulletin de l'IFAN* 11 (1949): 458–70.

Leriche, Albert, and Mokhtar Ould Hamidoun. "Notes sur le Trârza: Essai de géographie historique." *Bulletin de l'IFAN* 10 (1948): 461–538.

Levtzion, Nehemia. "Merchants vs. Scholars and Clerics in West Africa: Differential and Complementary Roles." In *Rural and Urban Islam in West Africa,* ed. Nehemia Levtzion and H. J. Fisher. Boulder, CO: Lynne Rienner, 1987, 21–38.

Lydon, Ghislaine. *On Trans-Saharan Trails: Islamic Laws, Trade Networks, and Cross-Cultural Exchange in Nineteenth-Century Western Africa.* Cambridge, UK: Cambridge University Press, 2009.

Machado, João Pedro. *Influência arábica no vocabulário português.* 2 vols. Lisbon: Álvaro Pinto, 1958–61.

Mark, Peter. *"Portuguese" Style and Luso-African Identity: Precolonial Senegambia, Sixteenth–Nineteenth Centuries.* Bloomington: Indiana University Press, 2002.

Marty, Paul. *L'émirat des Trarzas.* Paris: Éditions Ernest Leroux, 1919.

———. *Études sur l'Islam et les tribus Maures: Les Brakna.* Paris: Éditions Ernest Leroux, 1921.

Mauny, Raymond. "L'expédition marocaine d'Ouadane (Mauritanie) vers 1543–1544." *Bulletin de l'IFAN* 11 (1949): 129–40.

———. *Tableau géographique de l'Ouest Africain au Moyen Âge d'après les sources écrites, la tradition et l'archéologie.* Mémoires de l'Institut Français d'Afrique Noir, no. 61. Dakar: IFAN, 1961.

McDougall, E. Ann. "Research in Saharan History." *Journal of African History* 39 (1998): 467–80.

Mendes, António de Almeida. "Esclavages et traites ibériques entre Méditerranée et Atlantique (XVe–XVIIe siècles)." Thèse de doctorat mention "Histoire et Civilisations." Paris: École des Hautes Études en Sciences Sociales, 2007.

Monod, Théodore. *L'ile d'Arguin (Mauritanie): Essai historique*. Lisbon: Centro de Estudos de Cartografia Antiga do Instituto de Investigação Científica e Tropical, 1983.

Neto, Francisco Luis. "Carta de Francisco Luis Neto ao Conde de Castanheira." Arquivo Nacional da Torre do Tombo (Lisboa), *Colecção de S. Vicente*, livro 5, fls. 144–47 v, 1552.

Norris, H. T. "Sanhajah Scholars of Timbuctoo." *Bulletin of the School of Oriental and African Studies* 30 (1967): 634–40.

———. "Znaga Islam During the Seventeenth and Eighteenth Centuries." *Bulletin of the School of Oriental and African Studies* 32 (1969): 496–526.

———. *Saharan Myth and Saga*. Oxford: Clarendon, 1972.

———. "The Legacy of the Banu Hassan." *Maghreb Review* 2 (1977): 21–25.

———. *The Berbers in Arabic Literature*. Beirut: Librarie du Liban, 1982.

———. *The Arab Conquest of Western Sahara: Studies of the Historical Events, Religious Beliefs and Social Customs Which Made the Remotest Sahara a Part of the Arab World.* Harlow: Longman; Beirut: Librarie du Liban, 1986.

Ould al-Bara, Yahya. *La propriété foncière en Mauritanie: Dimensions sócio-politiques*. Rabat: Institut des Etudes Africaines de l'Université Mohamed V, 1999. In Arabic.

Ould Cheikh, Abdel Wedoud. *Eléments d'histoire de la Mauritanie*. Nouakchott: Centre Culturel Français Antoine de St. Exupéry, 1991.

———. "Herders, Traders and Clerics: The Impact of Trade, Religion and Warfare on the Evolution of Moorish Society." In *Herders, Warriors and Traders: Pastoralism in Africa,* ed. John Galaty and Pierre Bonte. Boulder, CO: Westview, 1991, 199–218.

———. "La caravane et la caravelle: Les deux âges du commerce à l'Ouest Saharien." *L'Ouest Saharien* 2 (1999): 29–70.

Ould Hamidoun, Mokhtar. *Précis sur la Mauritanie*. Saint-Louis du Sénégal: IFAN, 1952.

Ould Saʿad, Muḥammad al-Mukhtar. "Emirats et espace émiral maure: Le cas du Trarza aux XVIIIe–XIX siècles." *Revue du Monde Musulman et de la Méditerranée* 54 (1989): 53–82.

Ricard, R. 1936. "Le commerce de Berbérie et l'organisation économique de l'empire portugais aux XVe et XVIe siècles." *Annales de l'Institut d'Etudes Orientales d'Alger* 2 (1936): 266–90.

Rosales, Cristovão Valle de. "Carta de Cristovão de Rosales dando parte ao Rei da rúina em que estava o castelo de Arguim, motivo porque os castelhanos das Canárias iam ali resgatar a seu salvo, pedindo ao dito senhor lhe mandasse um caravelão porque junto com outros que tinha intimidariam os castelhanos." Arquivo Nacional da Torre do Tombo (Lisbon), *Corpo Cronológico*, parte I, mç. 82, no. 86, 1549.

Rosales, Pedro Valdez. "Carta de Pedro Valdez Rosales, governador do castelo de Arguim, expondo ao rei que, por falta de roupas, principal objecto daquele resgate, estava perdido o negócio daquele castelo de, que se aproveitavam os mercadores judeus trazendo-as de Tagos e fazendo o dito resgate." Arquivo Nacional da Torre do Tombo (Lisbon), *Corpo Cronológico*, parte I, mç. 86, no. 126, 1551.

Santana Pérez, Germán. "Arguin y Canarias durante la etapa moderna (siglos XV–XVIII)". In *Culturas del litoral: Dinámicas fronterizas entre Canarias y la costa sahariano-mauritana,* ed. Alberto López Bargados and Jesús Martínez Milán. Barcelona: Edicions Bellaterra, 2010, 45–65.

Saunders, A. C. d. C. M. "The Depiction of Trade as War as a Reflection of Portuguese Ideology and Diplomatic Strategy in West Africa, 1444–1556." *Canadian Journal of History* 17 (1982): 219–34.

Searing, James F. *West African Slavery and Atlantic Commerce: The Senegal River Valley, 1700–1860.* Cambridge, UK: Cambridge University Press, 2003 (1993).

Stewart, Charles. *Islam and Social Order in Mauritania: A Case Study from the Nineteenth Century.* Oxford: Clarendon, 1973.

Taine-Cheikh, Catherine. *Dictionnaire ḥassaniyya-français*. 7 vols. Paris: Geuthner, 1988–90.

———. "Les langues comme enjeux identitaires." *Politique Africaine* 55 (1994): 57–65.

———. *Dictionnaire zénaga-français*. Cologne: Rüdiger Köppe Verlag, 2008.

Taylor, Raymond. "Warriors, Tributaries, Blood Money and Political Transformation in Nineteenth-Century Mauritania." *Journal of African History* 36 (1995): 419–41.

———. "L'émirat précolonial et l'histoire contemporaine en Mauritanie." *Annuaire del'Afrique du Nord 1999* 38 (2002): 53–69.

Teixeira da Mota, A. "Viagens espanholas das Canárias à Guiné no século XVI, segundo documentos dos arquivos portugueses." *III Coloquio de Historia Canario-Americana.* Las Palmas 1978 Conference Proceedings, 1980.

Van Dantzig, A. *Forts and Castles of Ghana*. Accra: Sedco, 1980.

Villasante-De Beauvais, Mariella. *Parenté et politique en Mauritanie: Essai d'antropologie historique.* Paris: L'Harmattan, 1998.

Vogt, John. "The Lisbon Slave House and African Trade, 1486–1521." *Proceedings of the American Philosophical Society* 117 (1973): 1–16.

Webb, James L. A. *Desert Frontier: Ecological and Economic Change Along the Western Sahel (1600–1850).* Madison: University of Wisconsin Press, 1995.

———. "Ecology and Culture in West Africa." In *Themes in West Africa's History,* ed. E. K. Akyeampong. Athens: Ohio University Press; Oxford: James Currey; Accra: Woeli Publishing Services, 2006, 33–51.

Wehr, Hans. *A Dictionary of Modern Written Arabic.* Beirut: Librairie du Liban, 1980.

Whitcomb, Thomas. "New Evidence on the Origins of the Kunta-I." *Bulletin of the School of Oriental and African Studies* 38 (1975): 103–23.

———. "New Evidence on the Origins of the Kunta-II." *Bulletin of the School of Oriental and African Studies* 38 (1975): 403–17.

LANGUAGES OF ISLAM: HYBRID GENRES OF TAALIBE BAAY ORATORY IN SENEGAL

Joseph Hill
(American University in Cairo)
DOI: 10.5192/021540993020167

ABSTRACT

This paper shows how religious speeches by leaders of the Taalibe Baay, disciples of the Senegalese Sufi Shaykh Ibrahim Ñas, uphold Islamic knowledge and authority while accommodating competing yet intertwined knowledge regimes. French and Arabic enter into Wolof religious discourse in multiple ways through contrasting educational methods, uses, and language ideologies. These three languages are combined and separated in numerous linguistic registers juxtaposed in religious speeches: classical Arabic prologues and textual quotations, "deep Wolof" narratives largely excluding loanwords, more conversational registers using some French terms, and so on. Although orators typically use French terms sparingly, they sometimes break this pattern and use them liberally, especially when critiquing Western hegemony and secular values. They sometimes incorporate French discourses of "liberty" and "progress" in passages designed to demonstrate Islam's superiority in achieving these ideals. Orators tend to replace common French terms for morally positive concepts with Arabic terms, yet they usually reinsert the French as a gloss to facilitate comprehension. I discuss these utterances as cases of linguistic "hybridity" in which contrasting voices combine to serve an authorial purpose. These rhetorical patterns fit into a larger pattern of accommodating, contesting, and appropriating hegemonic languages, institutions, and ideas while upholding Islam's unique authoritativeness.

Islamic Africa, VOL. 2, NO. 1, 2011. ISSN 2154-0993.

Introduction

The fascination that Islamic and particularly Sufi authority in Senegal has long held for scholars hinges largely on the "exceptional" situation (Villalón 1995; Cruise O'Brien 1996) in which secular state authority simultaneously competes with and depends on informal Islamic governance. Despite a number of transformations eroding the sense of Sufi orders acting as monolithic blocs,[1] the vast majority of Senegalese[2] continue to look to Sufi leaders as the highest moral authorities and as metonyms of community. Sufi authority in Senegal has remained relevant through successfully accommodating multiple transformations and competing regimes—including multiple Islamic tendencies, secular state authority, and neoliberal development institutions—while remaining grounded in long traditions of religious scholarship, spiritual practice, and moral authority.

Islamic moral authority is constituted in relation to competing forms of authority in many settings. One of the most central yet overlooked of these is religious oratory in large meetings that many Sufi adherents attend regularly. This article suggests a homology between, on the one hand, word choice and register shifts in Taalibe Baay religious specialists' public speeches and, on the other, these specialists' more general orientation towards non-religious forms of knowledge and authority. The overall pattern that I suggest is that of acknowledging, engaging with, appropriating, criticizing, and ultimately subordinating alternative forms of knowledge and authority to uphold a particular imagination of Islamic knowledge and authority. Taalibe Baay orators' use of multiple languages and registers thus is part of a larger play of engagement and disengagement, "accommodation" and "resistance" (Robinson 2000), condescension and transcendence.

This analysis of language use is just one part of a larger project to understand the process of accommodation (Robinson 2000; Babou 2007) between religious and other forms of authority in Senegal. Over

---

[1] These include the decline of the Sufi orders' agrarian economic base (Diop 1993), the rise of transnationally connected Islamic reform movements (Loimeier 1994, 2000; Augis 2005, 2009; Leichtman 2009), and competing tendencies within Sufi movements (Kane and Villalón 1995; Villalón 2003; Samson 2005).

[2] According to the 2002 Senegal census (République du Sénégal 2002), approximately 90 percent of all Senegalese, or 94 percent of all Muslims in Senegal, identified with one of the primary Sufi orders.

the past decade, my ethnographic research on the "Taalibe Baay," or followers of the Senegalese Shaykh ʾIbrāhīm Ñas of the Tijānī Sufi order, has examined how Sufi discourses and practices negotiate mutually irreducible interests, imperatives, and truth claims. My research among Taalibe Baay began in their holy city, Medina Baay, which sits on the outskirts of the regional capital of Kaolack and is closely connected to the peanut-farming villages of Senegal's Saalum area. I soon extended my research to a number of other sites: several Saalum villages; Dakar, where the Taalibe Baay movement is booming among young people of all classes; an Arab village in Mauritania affiliated with the movement; Senegalese transmigrant communities in New York City; and Cairo, where many sons of Taalibe Baay leaders study at Al-Azhar University. This multi-sited approach has allowed me to observe how Taalibe Baay speak of various topics in numerous varieties of Wolof and other languages.

Although my research has followed Taalibe Baay around the world, it would be impossible to describe language patterns among Taalibe Baay globally, since the Taalibe Baay movement, known globally as the *Tijāniyyah ʾIbrāhīmiyyah* or the *Fayḍa*,[3] includes adherents who speak dozens of languages and live in nearly every country and setting, from remote Bedouin camps to large Western cities. Throughout this paper, the term "Taalibe Baay" refers to Wolof-speaking disciples of Baay Ñas in Senegal who actively participate in the religious community, often through membership in a religious association (*daayira*). This paper makes no attempt to define Taalibe Baay oratory as a distinct style or genre, as speakers' styles and linguistic repertoires vary and likely share common characteristics with speakers from other Sufi groups. However, the speeches examined here share a number of formal characteristics that justify approaching them as part of a set of "speech genres" (Bakhtin 1986) that combine registers according to more or less established patterns and expectations. All the orators whose speech I examine here are from prominent clerical families and are regular speakers on the Taalibe Baay meeting circuit. They have similar educational backgrounds, beginning

[3] Members of this movement generally refer to the movement growing out of Shaykh ʾIbrāhīm Ñas's teachings as the *Fayḍa* (Flood), although in Wolof individuals generally refer to themselves as "*Taalibe Baay,*" or "Disciples of Baay." Outsiders call them "Ñaseen" (the Ñas family) although this label is almost never used among members of the community. See Hill (2007) and Seesemann (2011).

in Senegalese Islamic schools (*daara* and majlis),[4] some passing through Mauritanian Bedouin schools, and culminating in a diploma from Al-Azhar University in Cairo. All regularly travel throughout Senegal and often abroad and are more or less conversant in urban and rural Wolof speaking styles. All have some knowledge of French and can draw on a range of French expressions regardless of whether they studied French or live primarily in an urban environment.

According to Bakhtin, all utterances take place in a context of "dialogized heteroglossia" (1981, 272), or in dialogue not only with other utterances but with multiple languages or ways of speaking. The oratorical genres employed in religious meetings are fundamentally heteroglossic, juxtaposing many speech registers and other genres: ancient classical Arabic prose, formalized Arabic poetry, Qurʾānic verses, "deep Wolof" narratives and translations, and conversational Wolof explanations incorporating many French loanwords. The only other academic account of Senegalese Islamic oratory that I know of, Kane and Villalón's (1995) translation and analysis of a controversial 1993 politico-religious speech by Moustapha Sy, suggests that such heteroglossia is by no means limited to Taalibe Baay. Although their translation does not preserve the details of loanwords and code-switching, it shows that this Tijānī leader consciously juxtaposes Arabic, French, and Wolof while discussing Islam's relationship to secular politics and modernity. A closer examination of Taalibe Baay speeches shows that they are not only heteroglossic but include "hybrid" utterances, or single utterances containing two utterances and thereby juxtaposing two opposing "axiological belief systems" (Bakhtin 1981, 304) while refracting them through a single authorial intent. Several speakers, using French terms, invoked Westerners' discourses advocating "women's liberation" and "equality" yet in such a way that casts doubt on the ability of secular liberalism to attain these goals.

In hybrid speech, it is often difficult to discern the speaker's intent among the many voices, many of which are invoked ironically to undercut the assumptions associated with those voices. Sufi leaders' statements are often designed to puzzle (Hill 2007; compare Fernandez 1980), and when I asked for clarifications, I was often told to seek the speaker's deeper (bāṭin)

[4] In this article I differentiate terms from the principal languages discussed by using different typefaces: *Wolof*, *Arabic*, and French. In my translations into English, I leave the Wolof in default typeface while setting apart Arabic and French as above, highlighting Wolof terms where needed using boldface.

meaning, which was often at odds with the apparent (*ẓāhir*) meaning (Hill 2007). Among the most puzzling aspects of these speeches was their extensive use of French phrases at certain moments, often after twenty minutes or more of scrupulously pure Wolof. I had expected these erudite Islamic scholars to assert Arabic, the language of Islamic scholarship, and Wolof, their own mother tongue, against French, the language of colonialism and modern, secular life. I have often encountered the attitude in Senegal that extensive use of French indexes a speaker's social attributes, whether positive (modern, urbane, cosmopolitan, or educated) or negative (overly Westernized or pretentious). Yet religious orators sometimes used a plethora of French terms in diatribes against the encroachment of anti-religious, Western values. In heteroglossic and hybrid speech, certain voices index not the speaker's identity but stereotyped personae (Agha 1998) invoked to undermine the very assumptions associated with them. Although it is impossible to comment on the degree to which speakers consciously and strategically consider each word while speaking, these hybrid discourses have a consistent rhetorical effect of appropriating and undermining non-religious knowledge regimes in order to uphold Islamic authority. My use of the term "regimes" derives from Foucault's discussion of "truth regimes," or "general politics" of how certain discourses are accepted as true (1984, 73). Yet while Foucault assumes that "each society has its regime of truth" (1984, 73), postcolonial Senegal is shaped by multiple epistemic traditions and centers of authority vying for hegemony.

French and Arabic in a Hybrid Wolof Linguistic Space

The religious oratory discussed in this paper thus takes place in a context where no single model of knowledge and authority is hegemonic, and this plurality is reflected in a multiplicity of languages and registers associated with different specializations, classes, and knowledge traditions. Wolof has functioned as a lingua franca in much of northwestern Senegal since the fifteenth century (Klein 1968), and its spread has accelerated since the mid-twentieth century to the point that at least 90 percent of Senegalese now speak it as a first or second language (McLaughlin 2008). While Wolof speakers today typically have difficulty identifying regional dialects, they easily distinguish between "Urban Wolof" and the "rural Wolof" spoken primarily by ethnic Wolof in villages (Juillard et al. 1994). As a number of scholars have shown, the contemporary Urban Wolof of Dakar is a "mixed code" in which French often acts less as a foreign language than as an integral part of a hybrid code even for those who have never studied French (Thiam 1990, 1994; Swigart 1992a, 1994; McLaughlin 2001, 2008). Indeed, Swigart (1992a, 1994) has demonstrated that many speakers, including politicians giving speeches, insist that they are speaking "pure" Wolof even as they observably engage in substantial "code-switching" (as defined from an outsider's perspective) and borrowing from French. Furthermore, urban speakers who have not studied French are often unaware of the French origin of many everyday terms (Swigart 1992b, 1994). This suggests that Urban Wolof discourse is a "hybrid language" (Spitulnik 1998) in which French expressions are often "bivalent," or belonging simultaneously to two languages (Woolard 1998; Swigart 2000; McLaughlin 2001). While we may think of registers as subsets of a language, code-switching between distinct languages or "grammatical systems" (Gumperz 1977) is a distinctive feature of Urban Wolof registers.

Although speakers may not be conscious of particular instances of "non-purposive" (Swigart 1994) code-switching, whether and how one uses French phrases is not always inconsequential. Depending on the social milieu, an abundance of French terms can mark a speaker as erudite, a parvenu, or not truly Senegalese (a *tubaab* [Westerner], as some returned expatriates are called). Conversely, a Wolof utterance that lacks French terms or insists on grammatical distinctions such as noun classes (Irvine 1978; McLaughlin 1997) may mark a "deep Wolof" (*Wolof bu xóot*) register suggesting the voice either of an uneducated peasant or a public speaker—an Islamic specialist, a griot (*géwal*),[5] or a radio or television announcer (Papa Alioune Ndao and Kébé 2010). Islamic scholars whose deep Wolof seems perfectly eloquent over the loudspeakers of a nocturnal religious meeting report being treated as ignorant peasants when they travel to Dakar.

Despite this mutually defining relationship between Senegal's official language and its lingua franca, a "diglossic" (Ferguson 1959) approach assuming a unified "linguistic market" and a state-sponsored "legitimate language" (Bourdieu 1991) would fail to capture the complexity of Senegal's linguistic landscape (Irvine 1989; Swigart 2000). A heteroglossic approach sees Wolof as an intersection between many languages, both

[5] "Griot" is the French term designating members of endogamous occupational groups specializing in praise singing, music, oral history, and relaying speeches to an audience. The most common Wolof word to designate members of such groups is *géwal*, although Wolof speakers who perform similar functions use a range of terms to designate themselves.

conventionally defined (French, Arabic, Wolof, English, and so on) and "social languages" (Bakhtin 1981). Research on contemporary Wolof speech has so far described only a limited number of these registers encountered in everyday speech and, to a lesser extent, in the specialized speech of griot wordsmiths (for example Irvine 1989; Heath 1990).

Studies attempting to situate Arabic within the Wolof linguistic landscape have shown that Arabic, like French, has provided numerous loanwords (Deme 1995) and sometimes serves as an alternative to French to align speakers with Islam and against Western hegemony (Ngom 2002, 2003). Yet the handful of Arabic terms used in everyday conversation are largely limited to stock greetings, the days of the week, and terms of religious significance, and many speakers are unaware of the Arabic origin of Arabic loanwords (Swigart 2000).[6] Moreover, as discussed below, the vast majority of terms associated with Islam—including the words for Muslim (*jullit*), prayer (*julli*), four of the five prayers themselves, and the feasts (*tabaski* and *korite*)—are unrelated to their Arabic equivalents. Some intellectuals and media personalities replace French terms with Arabic equivalents as an act of resistance, yet few have found this approach useful since few understand the resulting language (Swigart 1994, 181).

This situation raises important questions: Why has Arabic, the only widespread written language in Senegal throughout much of the past millennium, had little influence on the Wolof lexicon while French, little known in most of Senegal before the past century, is so at-home in everyday Wolof conversation? Why have Senegalese voluntarily adopted the language of the alien colonizer while apparently spurning that of Islam, the basis of Senegal's most powerful social associations? Why do Wolof speakers so often associate Islam with Wolof rather than with Arabic, as scholars such as Swigart (2000) argue, even though most of them have spent years memorizing Islam's holy book in its original language and pray in Arabic each day?

Answering these riddles requires considering how languages accompany contrasting pedagogical techniques, pragmatic uses, and language ideologies. Extending our analysis beyond everyday conversational registers, we see that Arabic is indeed a far more integral

[6] This is especially true of non-religious words derived from Arabic, including *saa* (moment, from *sāʿah,* "hour"); *waxtu* (hour, from *waqṭ,* "time"); *batañc* (eggplant, from *bādhinjān*); etc. The origin of some French-derived words is also generally forgotten, such as *mbalit* (trash, residual form of "*bale*" [balayer], meaning "residue from sweeping").

and ubiquitous part of everyday life in Senegal than studies of language in Senegal suggest. Perceiving this fact requires taking into account religious meetings, chants, cassettes of religious speeches, cell phone ring tones, Qurʾānic studies, prayers, and so on. Even to those who know little of Arabic grammar, Arabic discourses are more than mere background noise: they are mnemonic tools and techniques for cultivating and performing morality, community, authority, and religious subjectivity. However, Arabic terms appear less frequently in conversational Wolof, not only because Arabic is a specialized tool for religious instruction and worship, but because long-standing Arabo-Islamic instruction methods raise a lexical barrier between Arabic and Wolof that conceals the significant impact of Arabo-Islamic learning.

Among Taalibe Baay communities I have frequented in Kaolack, nearby Saalum villages, and Dakar, education in Qurʾānic schools (*daara*)[7] is nearly universal among boys and girls. The exercise of writing a text every day using Arabic characters has taught most people in these communities to read and write in Arabized Wolof (*ʿajamī* or *Wolofal*), yet a smaller number can write in romanized Wolof,[8] French, or Arabic.[9] This near-universal Wolof literacy is invisible to the postcolonial state.[10] In post-Qurʾānic schools (*majlis*),[11] one memorizes Arabic texts in the teacher's home, yet one typically studies and discusses these Arabic texts in Wolof.[12] Language immersion, a key ingredient of France's technology

---

[7] From Arabic "*dār al-Qurʾān*" or "house of the Qurʾān."

[8] "Romanized Wolof" includes both writing following French conventions and writing following the phonemic conventions of the CLAD (Centre de Linguistique Appliqué de Dakar).

[9] Irvine (1989) also noted that more people in the village she studied could write in Arabized Wolof and Arabic than French, although this was changing as state schools became more prominent.

[10] The 1988 Senegalese census (Sénégal 1988) reported that 28.6 percent of Senegalese men were literate in French, 6.5 percent in Arabic, and only 0.3 percent in national languages such as Wolof and Pulaar. It reported that 15.6 percent of women were literate in French, 1.2 percent in Arabic, and 0.2 percent in national languages. These outlandishly low figures for both Arabic and national languages reflect a number of assumptions, including that everyone is either illiterate or literate in exactly one language (as the total is 100 percent) and likely that literacy in national languages only includes romanized systems.

[11] Literally "a place of sitting" or "assembly."

[12] A growing number of Arabic schools, many of them funded partially by the state, use language immersion and "modern" methods patterned after Francophone schools, yet the religious orators discussed in this paper all began their studies in the "traditional" schools described here.

of assimilation first used to integrate France's multilingual citizenry and then in the colonies (Weber 1976; Johnson 2004), is absent from *majlis*.

An anecdote will illustrate how *majlis* affect one's linguistic repertoire. A fifteen-year-old *majlis* student, Sheex, has spent the day helping his teacher oversee nearly a hundred younger students as they memorize the Qurʾān at Sëriñ Daara Ibra's *daara* in the Taalibe Baay holy city of Medina Baay. The youngest students begin by learning the letters of the Arabic alphabet by their Wolof names[13] and then repeat very simple Qurʾānic phrases in unison as the rest of the students rock back and forth and recite the Qurʾānic verses they have written on wooden tablets. After the late afternoon prayer, the Qurʾān students are dismissed and Sheex stays behind at the *daara*, which consists of a low zinc roof surrounded by three cement-block walls within the teacher's compound. For the next hour he reviews the lesson that Sëriñ Daara Ibra gave him to memorize the previous night, which he has copied into his notebook, and then he joins the teacher in his bedroom.

Sëriñ Daara and I both sit atop the teacher's bed as Sheex kneels on an imported red prayer rug facing his teacher while bowing his head toward the ground. The teacher tells Sheex to begin reciting his lesson, a passage from Al-Akhḍarī, a book of *fiqh* or Islamic jurisprudence written in rhymed verse to facilitate memorization. Today's lesson concerns the proper execution of ritual prayer, or *ṣalāh*. Sheex recites the Arabic text from memory, careful to speak clearly yet softly out of deference for his teacher, and the teacher listens intently and stops Sheex occasionally to correct him. Sëriñ Daara congratulates Sheex on a good recitation and then tells him to recite it again, this time with the Wolof gloss. Sheex begins again, this time following each Arabic word with a deep Wolof equivalent. This form of recitation breaks up the verse's rhythm, drawing attention to each bilingual pair of equivalent words. The teacher then has Sheex repeat the Arabic-Wolof text once more, this time stopping Sheex periodically to interject his own commentary (*sharḥ*) in conversational Wolof, offering

[13] Many of the Wolof names describe the letter's appearance instead of or in addition to its sound. This is because Wolof speakers often collapse several Arabic phonemes into a single Wolof phoneme, in which case letters need further differentiation (see Ndiaye 1985, 44–45). For example, the Arabic letter *mīm* is called "*miimara*" in Wolof (from "*mīm rāʾ*" for "*mīm* in the shape of *rāʾ*"), while the Arabic letter *ḥāʾ* is called "*haa lonk*" or "*ḥāʾ* with a tail" to distinguish it from non-emphatic *hāʾ*, which most Wolof speakers do not differentiate from *ḥāʾ*.

examples of things that might go wrong during a prayer. At one point Sëriñ Daara stands up and acts out an imam forgetting the words of the Qurʾānic passage he is reciting during the prayer, then asks Sheex what the text prescribes to be done in this situation.

Nearly all the male Islamic specialists I interviewed or heard speak had studied at such *daara* and *majlis* in this fashion. Sons of better-known leaders typically went on to study at Al-Azhar in Egypt, while members of less prominent families like Sëriñ Daara combined study at various *majlis* with several years at formal Islamic institutes, whose methods resemble those of Francophone schools. Many boys from Taalibe Baay clerical families now study in Mauritanian villages affiliated with Baay Ñas. Most of the Arabic texts memorized in *majlis* are centuries-old verse texts that, like Al-Akhḍarī, are part of a canon studied throughout West Africa (Ndiaye 1985; Sule and Starratt 1991). These elliptical Arabic verses would be of little use without the Wolof gloss and the teacher's commentary. Because no immersion is involved, *majlis* students need many years to become conversant in Arabic, although they quickly learn many Arabic religious and grammatical terms. These schools' effect on students' Wolof lexicon is directly opposite to that of Francophone schools. While Francophone schools banish Wolof and thus encourage students to replace it with French, *majlis* teach students an ever-expanding body of deep Wolof glosses for specialized Arabic terms, allowing them to discuss the fine points of Islamic law and monotheistic theology with minimal borrowing from Arabic. This education teaches students of Islam to speak a deep Wolof with an unusually broad Wolof lexicon and conservative grammar resembling the speech of praise singers. Partly because prominent Islamic specialists have typically memorized dozens of long texts in both Arabic and Wolof, a Wolof specialist in Kaolack I hired to help me transcribe interviews visited Islamic leaders regularly, describing them as the best source of little-known Wolof vocabulary.

By contrast, not only are contemporary and high-prestige domains such as commerce, technology, politics, and international relations taught in French, but the methods used to teach French terms do not bundle them with Wolof equivalents. Centuries after the translation of terms used in Arabic texts into Wolof, efforts to Wolofize vocabulary introduced through Francophone channels (for example Diop 1979, chap. 2) have gained little traction. I encountered *majlis* students who could discuss religious topics in fluent Arabic yet had to resort to French for basic terms such as “politics” and “technology” (terms absent from canonical pedagogical texts) while speaking Arabic. In short, in everyday situations, even people who identify with Islamic knowledge often take for granted that the French way of saying something is the “unmarked” (Myers-Scotton 1995) or even the only way of saying it.

However, the taken for granted comes to the fore when a state of affairs changes. Religious specialists and students who migrated from Medina Baay to Dakar often felt a pressing need to learn to incorporate French into their Wolof. Sëriñ Daara Ibra spends several months each year in Dakar, where he exchanges mystical cures and religious knowledge with religious specialists there. A respected teacher and religious scholar in Medina Baay, he explained to me that when he first arrived in Dakar people treated him like an uneducated peasant. He traded religious lessons for French lessons with friends in Dakar and studied public school textbooks until he could pass the exam for the elementary and then the intermediary diploma. When speaking with me and other urbanites in Dakar he made a point of using French extensively, although he tended to switch between full sentences of pure Wolof and pure but halting French rather than code-mix spontaneously and intrasententially as do fluent Urban Wolof speakers. My young friends in Medina Baay who finished high school and went on to pursue a higher education in Dakar similarly went through an uncomfortable period during which they avidly learned which Wolof words to replace with French words. Like Sëriñ Daara Ibra, some began by speaking in full sentences of school-book French and only gradually learned to borrow French in more subtle ways that did not mark them as “lames” (Labov 1973).

More prominent religious leaders’ Islamic studies and experiences abroad both extend their linguistic repertoires and make them far more aware of borrowing and code-switching than many who have only experienced living in Dakar. Well-known religious leaders, including those whose speeches are examined below, have more experience in Dakar and are more comfortable speaking in Urban Wolof than Sëriñ Daara Ibra, although in private conversation they tend to speak the Wolof of contemporary Kaolack, which uses French vocabulary to discuss many fields but almost none of the extended code-switching so common in Urban Wolof. In addition to their education in Senegalese *majlis,* which has taught them the same “deep Wolof” register that Sëriñ Daara Ibra speaks, many prominent clerics continued their studies in Mauritanian desert schools[14] and at Al-Azhar University in Cairo. Exposed to Arabic newspapers and satellite television channels, they fluently speak Classical and Modern Standard Arabic in addition to Mauritanian and Egyptian dialects. Although Al-Azhar graduates borrow limited Arabic while speaking with non-specialist Senegalese, Al-Azhar students I have observed in Cairo replace many French loanwords with Arabic equivalents, just as Senegalese transmigrants in New York do with English. While many French loans are "integrated" (Thiam 1994) enough to persist across urban, rural, and emigrant Wolof varieties, other terms occupy a "foreign" slot that speakers fill with terms from the official language of their milieu. Yet when they return to Senegal, these Wolof speakers must switch back to the mostly Wolof-French code that most of their interlocutors understand.

In this heteroglossic linguistic context, Taalibe Baay orators draw on multiple linguistic resources to relate Islamic knowledge to contemporary situations shaped by competing regimes of knowledge and legitimacy. Enabled by multilingual education and experience, yet constrained by their audience's limited shared linguistic repertoire, these religious specialists engage in subtle code-switching, borrowing, and glossing, refracting multiple social languages through a single, hybrid linguistic performance. In these performances, French and Arabic do not always act as monolithic wholes. Sometimes they are unmarked parts of everyday conversational registers; sometimes they stand in for civilizational binaries of Western hegemony and Islamic moral authority; and sometimes their conspicuous absence marks a shift to a weighty, deep Wolof register.

To Gloss or Not to Gloss: Moral and Political Implications

One of the most striking and widespread attributes of religious oratory I have observed is speakers' tendency in certain registers to deliver the same content in more than one language, usually in Arabic followed by French or, less commonly, Wolof. I have never observed this practice in informal conversations, where the French term would be used if non-Islamic specialists are present and an Arabic term might be used among only Islamic specialists. Because this glossing practice does not change the utterance's locutionary effect or literal meaning, this phenomenon only

[14] In Mauritania, the equivalent to Senegalese *majlis* is called the *maḥẓara*, which uses similar methods except that due to the similarity between classical Arabic and the Mauritanian dialect (*Ḥassāniyya*), the words are not repeated in the local language.

makes sense in terms of its perlocutionary or rhetorical effect. It would be impossible to determine an oratorical utterance's range of intentions and effects. Rather, the purpose here is to describe recurring patterns demarcating the principal registers used in religious oratory and to identify some rhetorical implications of particular language practices within these registers.

All the speeches I have transcribed and analyzed here are keynote speeches from large gatherings by major male leaders in their late fifties and sixties. As mentioned above, all had spent several years studying at Al-Azhar, and all either live permanently or spend several months a year in Dakar. All have acquired a working knowledge of French, although none have studied extensively in Francophone schools. An analysis of speeches by younger, rural, or female Islamic specialists would likely reveal different language patterns, although I have observed similar linguistic practices among different categories of speakers.[15] These speakers typically do not phonologically Wolofize French loanwords and are capable of almost completely removing them from certain registers, showing that they are more or less aware of the origins of the words they use, whether or not they consciously think of each particular word's origin as they use it. Most of the gloss patterns described in this section occur during segments that employ a more conversational register and address contemporary issues as opposed to the deep Wolof segments addressing issues of Islamic learning and history. When speaking about these religious issues, they draw on an extensive deep Wolof vocabulary acquired largely through their <u>*majlis*</u> education. Deep Wolof is used in everything from short, narrative illustrations in a more conversational conference speech to a full, single-register speech such as a *gàmmu* [<u>*mawlid*</u>] narrative relating the life of the Prophet Muḥammad. When discussing contemporary issues, speakers make little attempt to stick to the "pure" Wolof neologisms widespread in broadcast journalism (Ndao and Kébé 2010).

Unglossed French Terms vs. "Deep" Wolof

Well-known Taalibe Baay orators are mostly likely to use French terms where there is no widely used Wolof equivalent, although occasionally

[15] Thiam (1994), for example, establishes significant variations in code-switching and borrowing by class, gender, and education among Dakar Wolof speakers. Hill (2010) discusses female Taalibe Baay leaders' rhetorical strategies.

a French term where they might have used a Wolof term merely marks a conversational register. While they do not hesitate to "borrow" from French, unlike most Urban Wolof speakers, they rarely "codeswitch" (Myers-Scotton 1992) for longer phrases or clauses. However, during certain parts of speeches, especially those relating to contemporary problems, they use French loanwords liberally. When speaking in such a conversational register, speakers are likely to use a French term without preceding it with its Arabic equivalent under one or more of the following conditions:

1. The term is widely used and therefore unmarked as a foreign term.
2. It lacks a positive moral or religious connotation.
3. It is associated with a "modern" field (mechanics, politics, bureaucracy, mass media) introduced during or since French colonialism.

When speaking in a more conversational register, orators are very likely to use French for several categories of terms. The following examples represent a smattering of unglossed French terms I recorded in religious speeches:

- Technology, science, and medicine: freiner (brake), pneus (tires), ordinateur (computer), ulcère, hypertension, ordonnance (prescription), hôpital, clinique, salle d'accouchement (maternity room)
- Temporal terms (before/after, temporal units, months), especially when involving numbers.
- Geography: most countries and cities, even Arabic-speaking ones. Possible exceptions: neighboring Mauritania (*Gànnaar*). The world (monde) in a spatial/global sense, yet the Wolofized Arabic term *àddina* (from *Ad-dunyā*) in a cosmic/moral sense.
- Numbers above ten, including years (whether Gregorian or *Hijra*), prices, distances. One to ten are often in Wolof. The number and accompanying noun agree in language: *ñaari fan* (two days) but trente-cinq jours (thirty-five days).
- Urban objects and places: building, apartment, neighborhood, floor, elevator, and accompanying ordinal numbers (deuxième étage [second floor]).
- Modern institutions and society (développement, loi, évolution, milieu, société, sondage [survey], parlement, Président de la Republique, domaine, marchandise, dépenser [spend], absenté, divorcer, preuve)

- Organizations (réunion, conférence, congrès, organisation, organiser, séminaires, président, secrétaire, trésorier, fédération, agenda, calendrier)
- Academics (sociologie, science politique, anthropologie, culture, intellectuels, thèse, lire); disciplines long established in the Islamic world can go either way (histoire/*tārīkh;* géographie/*jughrafiyyah;* philosophie/*falsafah*).
- French terms well integrated into Wolof (reposer [to rest], efforts, souhaiter [wish], garanti, lettre, répétition, rôle, reconnaître [recognize], respecter).
- Connecting words (parce que; sinon; cependant; mais; en plus; tu vois).
- Phrases of foreign origin (société Islamique, libération de la femme).

In any of these cases in conversational Wolof, the French term would be at least as unobtrusive as a Wolof equivalent. As Islamic orators by default use far fewer French words than most urban Senegalese, using a French word where a Wolof word would serve just as well may have ideological overtones. Although most uses of French words are non-purposive, the use of French after a very long stretch of deep Wolof often occurs during moments when speakers are appropriating or criticizing certain moral values from an Islamic position. There are several possible causes, including linguistic ideologies ascribing French negative moral connotations and the fact that modern social ills and secular ideologies are better known by their French names while religious values are taken from Arabic texts. For example, a speaker at a 2010 conference in Kaolack on "Women in Islamic Society," after an extended passage without any substantive French terms, suddenly spoke of the project of women's liberation:

> *Waaye nag ba Lislaam ñëwee, Yàlla ci boppam wàcce Alquraan* libérer *jigéen ñi jox* drapeau *moomu Yónent u Yàlla Muḥammad ṣallā Allāhu ʿalayhī wa-sallam. Damay wax ne mashrūʿ bu mag ci* liberté*-i jigéen kii nga xam ne moo indiwoon* drapeau *mooy Yónent u Yàlla Muḥammad ṣallā Allāhu ʿalayhī wa-sallam.*
>
> But when Islam came, God himself sent down the Qurʾān and liberated women and gave that banner to the Prophet *Muḥammad, may God pray over him and bless him*. I say that the great *project* of women's liberty, the one who brought the banner was the Prophet *Muḥammad, may God pray over him and bless him.*[16]

[16] Talk by Abdul Baaqi Dem, Lewna Ñaseen Kaolack, June 12, 2010.

The speaker refracts the language of liberal feminism through a speech that describes "feminist movements" as part of a well-financed Western plot against Islam. Such hybridity is absent from deep Wolof passages commenting on classical texts or dealing with solemn questions set apart from contemporary politics. For example, during a sober apostrophe to Baay Ñas that culminated a speech at a *gàmmu* (*mawlid*) dedicated to Ñas, Baay's son Baaba Lamin stated:[17]

> *Ñoo daje fii, di la fàtteliku,* ***ngir*** *mën a* ***jëfandikoo*** *lim daan dénk*
>
> We gather here to remember you, *in order to* be able to *use* what he [God] entrusted.

By contrast, even conservative speakers in a conversational register would certainly use more French words, for example:

> *Ñoo daje fii, di la fàtteliku* (or souvenir), **pour** *ñu mën a* **utiliser** *lim daan dénk.*

Such a weighty moment called for language set apart from everyday banter and thus in a deep Wolof register that excludes French loanwords.

Unglossed Arabic

Orators' use of Arabic contrasts in several ways from their use of French. Whereas they generally use French only in short words and phrases, they most often use Arabic in full sentences, opening each speech with a long, highly formalized, and untranslated Arabic prologue and then liberally punctuating their speeches with quotes from scripture and poetry that they then translate into deep Wolof. This prologue is obligatory and takes the same form as the prologue of any Islamic text.[18] It sometimes ends with an excuse for switching into Wolof, "the local dialect," for the

[17] Annual Gàmmu of Tayba Ñaseen, Baay Ñas's birthplace, July 2009.

[18] Prologues to speeches and texts are in highly classical Arabic and begin with "In the Name of God the Compassionate, the Merciful" and continue with prayers on the Prophet and his followers, etc. Whereas textual prologues end with "*ʾammā baʿd*" ("as for what follows"), a speech's prologue ends with a switch into Wolof and a (partly Arabic) greeting to the audience (for example, "*Mbokk yi, as-salāmu ʿalaykum*" ("*Fellow* [Muslims], *peace be upon you*").

sake of their audience. The transition to Wolof is usually marked by the phrase "*mbokk yi*" (fellow [Muslims/disciples]) and a formalized Wolof greeting to the audience and dignitaries. Also contrary to their use of French, which is rarely glossed into Wolof or Arabic, speakers gloss all but a few well-known Arabic terms and quotations. The short list of Arabic terms not requiring a gloss comprises almost exclusively Islamic terms generally known to the audience and having no well-known French or Wolof equivalent. Griots tend to be even more conservative than Islamic specialists about prohibiting Arabic terms from formal deep Wolof oratory. When relaying a patron's speech, they typically translate even well-known Arabic words into a Wolof equivalent (for example, rendering ẓāhir (apparent) as "*luy feeñ*" and bāṭin (inner) as "*luy nëbbu*").

As I have discussed, few Arabic words are needed to discuss Islamic subjects because many commonly used Islamic terms have etymologically unrelated or significantly modified Wolof equivalents. These include Muslim (*Jullit*), prayer (*julli*); fast (n: *koor*, v: *woor*); the names of four of the five daily prayers; a shaykh (*sëriñ*),[19] the names of the Islamic feasts (*korite*, *tabaski*); mosque (*jàkka*); Qur'ānic interpretation [tafsīr] (*piri*), to interpret (*firi*); and Prophet (*Yónent*). Additionally, many other Islamic terms significantly alter the pronunciation or meaning of many words of Arabic origin: Qur'ānic school (*daara*, from *dār al-Qur'ān* [house of the Qur'ān]); tablet (*àlluwa*, from *al-lūḥ*); religious association (*daayira*, from *dā'ira* [circle]); imam (*ilimaan*, from *āl-'Imam*); friday mosque (*jumaa*, from *masjid al-jumu'ah* [Friday mosque]);[20] Sufi (*suufiyànke*); pilgrimage (*àjji*, from *ḥajj*); pilgrim (*Àllaaji*, from *Al-Ḥājj* [m]; *Ajaa*, from *Al-Ḥājjah* [f]); religion (*diine*, from *dīn*); blessing (*barke*, from *barakah*); reward (*tuyaaba*, from *thawāb*); *sikkar* ([to repeat] the name of God; also a meeting where the *sikkar* is chanted, from *dhikr Allāh*, "mentioning God"; *tudde Yàlla* [to name God] in "pure Wolof"). The handful of Arabic terms that more or less maintain their Arabic form are mostly specialized Islamic/Sufi terms (*waẓīfah* [*wasifa*], *wird*, *ziyārah* [*siyaare*], *darajah*, *maqāmah*, *tarbiyah*).[21]

---

[19] This term has many meanings, only partially overlapping with the Arabic word *shaykh*, referring to an Islamic leader. In religious oratory, however, it has roughly the same meaning as *shaykh*.

[20] The term more often used in Arabic for Friday mosque is *masjid jāmi'*.

[21] "Islam" (*Lislaam*) itself is "bivalent" (Woolard 1998), potentially deriving from French "l'Islam" or Arabic "al-'Islām." Some speakers maintain the glottal stop, differentiating it from the French.

Some classical Arabic disciplines have conventional French glosses that orators often provide, for example, *naḥw* (grammaire) and *ṣarf* (conjugaison). However, orators may leave classical Arabic disciplines and terms of Islamic jurisprudence (*fiqh*) unglossed despite their obscurity (for example, *ʿiddah*, *mīrāth*) if their exact meaning is not essential to the author's point. For example, one speaker, narrating that people from around the world came to Baay seeking mystical knowledge that only he could dispense, said:

> *Jàngsiwuñ Al-Qurʾān; wutsiwuñ xam-xamu fiqh; jàngsiwuñ naḥw; jàngsiwuñ balāghah; jàngsiwuñ bayānī; jàngsiwuñ tafsīru l-Qurʾān.*[22]
>
> They didn't come to study *Al-Qurʾān;* they didn't come seeking knowledge of *fiqh* [jurisprudence]; they didn't come to study *naḥw* [grammar]; they didn't come to study *balāghah* [rhetoric]; they didn't come to study *bayānī* [diction]; they didn't come to study *tafsīru l-Qurʾān* [interpretation of the Qurʾān].

Here it is less important that the audience recognize all these disciplines than that they understand that none of them is Sufism. However, when emphasizing Baay Ñas's knowledge in various classical disciplines, the same speaker lists Ñas's books, in each case listing the Arabic discipline alongside a French gloss or Wolof explanation. In short, aside from a small number of widely known Islamic terms, speakers must gloss any Arabic terms they want their audience to understand. Arabic terms are therefore rarely used for convenience. The opposite is the case for French terms, which speakers use primarily where they provide the most convenient way to communicate with the audience.

Gloss Patterns and Linguistic Hierarchy

I have encountered the following distinct gloss patterns in Taalibe Baay religious oratory, in order of prevalence:

1. Arabic–French
2. Arabic–Wolof
3. Wolof–French
4. Wolof–Arabic or French–Arabic (uncommon)

---

[22] Mustafaa Géy, Gàmmu Baay in Jëppël, Dakar, 2004.

Each of these patterns accompanies distinct connotations and uses. By far the most common single-phrase gloss pattern is that of Arabic to French, followed by Arabic to Wolof and, less commonly, Wolof to French. In the vast majority of cases, then, the gloss proceeds from the language more associated with Islamic knowledge and authority to the language less associated with it: Arabic, Wolof, then French. In the few cases where Arabic comes second, this may be an inadvertent effect of the habit of using the French term. French is almost never glossed to Wolof, and indeed, far more common than all glosses together is the use of unglossed French terms. However, in deep Wolof passages sharply differentiated from contemporary informal discourse, terms widely understood to be of French origin almost completely disappear. For example, highly stylized *gàmmu* (*mawlid*) narratives stay from start to finish in a deep Wolof register, only using words of French origin that have completely lost any foreign implication (such as "*làmp*" [light]).

Speakers employ two ways to separate religious speech from conversational speech that ordinarily privileges French as a neutral lexical repository. The first, encountered above, is to replace French terms with Wolof equivalents, which may mark a deep Wolof register if used consistently. The second, especially prevalent when discussing more contemporary problems in a more conversational register, is to precede the French term with an Arabic equivalent, thus demoting the ordinarily unquestioned French term to the status of a gloss. Gloss patterns clearly privilege Arabic over Wolof and Wolof over French as a legitimate source of morally authoritative knowledge. Speakers are more likely to go to the effort of inserting an Arabic word followed by a gloss if the term has some moral, religious, or social implication, thus suggesting an association between such matters and Islamic knowledge/authority.

Distantly following Arabic–French, the second most common gloss pattern is Arabic–Wolof. Some of these glosses resemble Arabic–French glosses in replacing an expected French word with an Arabic word, except that they avoid the French altogether (in this case, the French word "famille"):

Ci turu ʿāʾilah bi, njabot gi. . . .

On behalf of the *family*, *the family*. . . .[23]

[23] Sëriñ Maamun Ibrayima Ñas, Gàmmu Baay in Tayba Ñaseen, 2004.

However, more often than to replace commonly used French terms, Arabic–Wolof glosses involve specialized Islamic terms that are not ordinarily named in French and are often closer to an explanation or definition than a mere gloss.

kooku ***sīra*** *la, muy* ***jaar-jaari yonent bi****.*

that [book] is ***sīra***, that is, the *doings of the Prophet.*[24]

In short, speakers in Taalibe Baay meetings tend to favor two main categories of Arabic terms: replacements for commonly used French terms, often those with positive moral or religious connotations; and specialized vocabulary from Islamic disciplines. In either case the Arabic term is usually glossed—in the first case into French and in the second into either Wolof or French. The habit of using Arabic terms first and then glossing them into more commonly understood French or Wolof extends occasionally to less morally charged adverbs and conjunctions.

Glosses follow several syntactic patterns. The most common is to append it to the Arabic word or the clause without a conjunction:

Mu hijra, immigrer *ba ñëw* Libie *ak* Tunisie.

He *immigrated*, immigrated to Libya and Tunisia. [*hijra:* religious connotation, recalls the Prophet Muḥammad's *hijra.*][25]

mu mel ni benn sharīṭ video—film cinema walla film vidéo

like a video *cassette*—a cinema film or a video film[26]

Qānūn al-Faransi—Constitution *bu* France

French law—constitution of France[27]

Occasionally the Arabic and French or Wolof gloss is joined by a "that is" or an "and" in Wolof instead of being simply appended:

qismu l-ʿālī, mooy enseignement supérieure

advanced division, that is, higher education[28]

---

[24] Mustafaa Géy, Gàmmu Baay in Jëppël, Dakar, 2004.

[25] Mustafaa Géy, Gàmmu Baay in Jëppël, Dakar, 2004.

[26] Muḥammad al-ʾAmīn (Baaba Lamin) Ñas, Gàmmu Baay, Tayba Ñaseen, 2005.

[27] Bashiir Ñas, conference in Dakar, 2005.

[28] Mustafaa Géy, Gàmmu Baay in Jëppël, Dakar, 2004.

Ay riḥla-am nag aki tukkéem

His *travels* and his travels[29]

nit u Qānūn la, mooy nit u loi

he's a person of *law*, that is, a person of law[30]

Occasionally, if the glossed term occupies a different syntactical place in Arabic than in French or Wolof, it may be placed in different parts of the sentence. For example, the word "even" in Arabic (*ḥattā*) and French (même) precedes the noun or clause but in Wolof (*sax*) follows it:

ḥattā *ba lenn ci ñoom* ***sax*** *. . .*

such that *even* one of them *even* . . .[31]

ḥattā bu de ab tubaab sax . . .

even if it's a European *even* . . .[32]

Même *turu baayam wim àmme* ***sax****, daf ciy génn dem ci turu jëk-këram. . . . Ḥattā sant baayam wi nga xam ne* ***sax*** *mooy cosaanam. . . .*

Even the name of her father that she possesses *even*, she leaves behind and goes to the name of her husband. . . . *Even* her father's surname *even* that is her heritage. . . .[33]

Note that in the last example, the first clause begins with the ubiquitous French word "*même*" ("even") and ends with the Wolof gloss (*sax*), while the second sentence repeats the same pattern but with the Arabic equivalent (*ḥattā*) instead of the French. This order, placing the habitual French word first and deliberate Arabic word second, is much less common. In each of these cases, the Wolof word (*sax*) is preceded by a semantically superfluous Arabic word (*ḥattā*), which occupies the same syntactic position as the French term, suggesting that the Arabic term was specifically inserted to displace the expected French term. This construction demonstrates that

[29] Mustafaa Géy, Gàmmu Baay in Jëppël, Dakar, 2004.

[30] Bashiiru Ñas, conference in Dakar, 2005.

[31] Bashiiru Ñas, conference in Dakar, 2005. In the same speech: "***Even*** those who went so far ***even*** as to say . . ." ("***Ḥattā*** *ñi nga xam ne dem nañ* ***sax*** *ba ne . . .*")

[32] Baaba Lamin Ñas, Gàmmu Baay, Tayba Ñaseen.

[33] Bashiiru Ñas, conference in Dakar, 2005.

Arabic often specifically serves to replace an unwanted French term, even if the term in question has no moral implication.

When an Arabic term follows its Wolof equivalent, its role is usually to supplement the Wolof word with a more precise Arabic meaning for the benefit of those with some knowledge of Arabic:

> *Danaa leen defal* synthèse *ci diggante—ʿalāqa Baay ak waa Naygīriyā.*
>
> I will give you a synopsis of the *relationship—relationship* between Baay and the people of *Nigeria*. ["Synopsis" (synthèse): commonly used word with no moral connotation; *Nigeria*: Arabic because their long-standing relationship is based on Islam, no need for gloss because it resembles the French equivalent; "Relationship" (*diggante*, *ʿalāqa*): common Wolof term, Arabic has moral/religious connotations.][34]

One of the most interesting and rare patterns is Wolof–French, which may seem counterintuitive as it appears to gloss a native term into a foreign one. During a formal *gàmmu* speech, one son of Baay Ñas used the rarely used Wolof word "*kuppe*," immediately appending its French equivalent, "football." This pattern allowed the speaker to remain in a deep Wolof register while making himself intelligible by glossing into conversational Wolof.

Far less common than Arabic–Wolof or Arabic–French is the French–Arabic pattern, which reverses the linguistic hierarchy. Cases I have observed may be double takes where the speaker uses a common French word by habit and then backtracks to give the Arabic equivalent:

> famille—*ʾusra* Ñaseen.
>
> The Ñaseen family—*family*.
>
> *Kooku* conjugaison *la, muy ṣarf.*
>
> That one [book] is conjugation, that is, *ṣarf*.[35]

Despite this handful of exceptions, the vast majority of glosses move clearly in the direction of Arabic–Wolof–French, or from the language of Islamic learning through the language whose "deep" speech is often associated with Islamic authorities to the language associated with colonialism, the state, and modern secular pursuits. This general tendency

[34] Mustafaa Géy, Gàmmu Baay in Jëppël, Dakar, 2004.

[35] Both quotes come from Mustafaa Géy's speech at the Gàmmu Baay in Jëppël, Dakar, 2004.

of upholding Arabic and Islamic knowledge in relation to French and its associated fields of knowledge is the background against which one can make sense of patterns that go against this tendency.

An Example of Hybridity and Hegemony

The patterns enumerated above are consistent with religious leaders' general tendency to privilege Islam in moral and religious matters while accommodating an environment shaped by a plurality of forms of knowledge and authority. Yet what do we make of situations where speakers break out of these patterns, privileging French where Wolof terms would be better understood, or vice versa? I explain these departures in terms of what Bakhtin (1981) calls "hybrid" utterances, which refract multiple voices and points of view through a single utterance, achieving an effect beyond what could be achieved with a straightforward statement of fact. When favoring French terms over Wolof terms, speakers often appropriate a "modern," "Western," "scientific," or "secular" voice to support an Islamic position. For example, speakers sometimes invoke scientific findings or human rights discourses to support Islam's rationality and justice and perhaps to point out modernity's or the West's failure to live up to the values they teach. Speakers often borrow a French term for negative moral attributes while using Arabic terms for positive attributes, thus associating decadence with the West and/or modernity and morality with Islam.

This section focuses on a speech given by Ustaas Bashiir Ñas, a well-known Taalibe Baay Arabic teacher who studied, like many other Taalibe Baay scholars, at Al-Azhar University in Cairo. He delivered this speech at a daytime conference in Dakar during Ramadan of 2005 hosted by a son of Baay Ñas, Maamun Ñas, on the theme of "The Woman and Development in Islam." Daytime conferences during Ramadan often have such "current issues" ("*actualités*") as their topic. Bashiir Ñas's speech illustrates deviations from the standard language patterns particularly well because, like many such conference speeches, it switches between deep Wolof narratives, direct quotations from the Qurʾān and other Arabic sources, more conversational religious exhortations, and politically charged discussions of Islam and modernity.[36]

The teacher's talk followed a shorter speech in French by a medical doctor, who justified his use of French saying, in Wolof:

[36] The speech consists of around two hours of content worthy of discussion in its own right, although such a discussion must wait for another occasion.

> Dama bëggoon ñu may ma tuuti ñu wax ci baatu Français, parce que du ñàkk ñu jël ko Internet te item journalistes yi pour ñu mën koo topp.
>
> I would like to be allowed to speak in the French language a little, because it [the conference] will certainly be taken to the Internet and also so that the journalists can follow it.

Giving the media something to report is among the primary purposes of any large meeting's opening segment, which functions as a point of engagement between the religious community, the state, the public sphere, and other entities. The main segment that follows is directed more specifically to the religious community. Bashiir Ñas's talk followed this French speech. As is typical of talks given by Islamic specialists on Islamic topics, he began with an Arabic prologue, in this case lasting one minute (much shorter than the prologues at larger religious events such as a *gàmmu*/*mawlid*), including the standard prayer on the Prophet, before switching to Wolof to greet the audience and expound on his topic.

The speaker introduced the topic of the conference using two French words placed in a Wolof clause—"the matter of women and development in Islam" ("*mbiram* femme *ak* développement *ci biir Lislaam*"). Over the past decade, "Women and Islam" has become one of the most common topics for Taalibe Baay and other Islamic conferences due to a number of local and global factors. Many of these conferences are organized or supported by womens' disciple associations, and a confluence of growing political attention to Muslim women and the focus of international institutions on "gender and development" have raised the profile of this question and led religious leaders both to respond to claims that Islam is oppressive to women and to appropriate "Western" discourses of liberty and equality to support Islam as a solution (Hill 2010).

Throughout his speech, Ñas favored Arabic words when expressing concepts of religious or positive moral significance, using them first and then following them where necessary with French or Wolof glosses:

> *Kaayleen ñu jël . . .* ***niqāṭ*** *yi,* ***tomb*** *yi ñiy teg ci ḥarf yi.*
>
> Come and let's take . . . the *dots,* the *dots* that we place on the *letters.* [*ḥarf* (letter, Wolof: *araf*): no need for gloss; *niqāṭ* (dots): evokes Arabic and religious texts.]

Ci kilifaab kanīsa bi la bokk, église *bi.*

He was one of the leaders of the *church,* the church. [There is no well-known Wolof equivalent.]

The Wolof portion of the speech began with a relatively high concentration of French terms as the speaker discussed what Western sociologists had said about the position of women in the modern West. When narrating modern, urban situations he used French terms liberally.

Although he sometimes used French to refer to legal and political terms known in the Senegalese context, he privileged Arabic terms in many places where ordinary conversation would call for a French term:

Nit u Qānūn la, mooy nit u loi.

He [an Arab lawyer] is a person of *law,* that is, a person of law.

Al-Qānūn al-Faransi, Constitution *bu* France.

French law, Constitution of France.

His source on French and English laws concerning women, which argued that the West has historically been less liberal toward women than Islam, was an Arabic book, whose technical terms he used even when a well-known French equivalent existed. Thus, following his Arabic source, he referred to the British House of Lords in Arabic (without gloss) as "*Majlis al-Lūrdāt.*"

The speaker's choice of language makes clear genealogies of academic knowledge. When referring to Arabic works, whether discussing Islamic history or European and American law and politics, he tends to use more Arabic terms, whether or not he is quoting directly or speaking of religious topics. When referring to Western sociological research (whether French or American), the speaker uses French terms. Interestingly, these segments use not only French technical terms but also French connecting words uncommon in religious discourse.

Moo tax ñuy sonder *kër yi waaye itam di* sonder *mbedd mi ndax mbedd mi itam* parti *la ci kër gi.*

That's why they survey houses but also survey the streets, because the street is part of the house.

> *Soo* analyser-*woon ca biiram,* sociologues *yi ñu ne,* perte *la loo xam ne su fekkee bim la koy wax mat na* 40 kilo, 50 kilo, *boo ko tegoon ci* balance *léegi matatul* 10 kilo. Et puis dessous *nga ko, maanaam, ñàkk na yaakaar ci yaw. . . . benn* sorte examin *la.*
>
> If you were to analyze deep down, the sociologists say, it's a loss that, [it's as if] if one were to tell you [something] weighs 40 kilos, 50 kilos, if you placed it on the *scale* now it weighs not even 10 kilos. And then you lowered her. . . . It's a kind of test.

During this portion of the talk, focusing on how the West has enslaved women while claiming to liberate them, Ñas used a large proportion of French connecting words and general, non-specialized vocabulary, his usage of French resembling that of Francophone-educated Dakar dwellers. However, even here he preceded many French terms, especially those with some positive religious or moral implications, with their Arabic equivalents. In many cases, rather than gloss a term immediately, he would use two parallel clauses, placing the Arabic term in one clause and then the French term in the next:

> *Amut haqq i toxal moomeelu alalam mu jëm ci keneen. Amut* droit *ci tayle alalam.*
>
> She has no *right* to *transfer ownership* of her possessions to someone else; she has no right to *mortgage* her wealth. (Note the Wolof legal terms.)
>
> *Ci* 18me *[siècle],* 1805, *Qānuun al-Biritānī: ci* Àngalteer *fii, seen* loi *yi, luñ wax?*
>
> In the 18th [century], 1805, *British Law,* in England here, their laws, what do they say?

He referred to "history" (an ancient discipline) with an Arabic-French gloss—"*tārīkh*—*histoire*"—but the modern field of "sociology" simply by its French name (*sociologie*). Note in the first of these two examples that he uses deep Wolof legal terms that he likely learned while studying Islamic jurisprudence (*fiqh*) texts in a *majlis*.

He occasionally used a phrase combining an unmarked French term with a more specialized Arabic term:

dañoo génn ci loi-*wu "tabīʿah,"* loi-*wu* nature *bi.*

they have departed from the law of *nature,* the law of nature.

But when using terms of religious significance, he avoided the French whenever possible, instead glossing Arabic into Wolof:

jigéen mbindéef la moo xam ne amul rūḥ, amul bakkan.

woman [before Islam] is a creation that has no *soul,* has no *soul.*

By contrast, when making a negative pronouncement about the West or other cultures (even Muslims or pre-Islamic Arabs), the speaker often used French terms, turning these normally neutral French words into ideological weapons:

dañoo jàpp ne jigéen benn outil *la.*

they take woman for a mere tool.

Léegi ndax jigéen war na jàng walla waruta jàng, ndax . . . ? Ignorance!

Now, should women study or not study, should . . . ? Ignorance!

Comportement *yu . . . góori jullit ñi baaxut* envers *jigéen ñi jullit ñi. . . .*
Seen mentalité, *seen* comportement *la, waaye Yàlla waxu ko.*

The behavior of . . . Muslim men toward Muslim women is not good. . . .
It's their mentality, their behavior, but God didn't say it.

Tubaab façon *bi ñuy* traiter, maltraîter *jigéen,*

Europeans' way of treating, mistreating women.

pas pour *ngeen taaj ñu, ñu doon ay* marchandise . . .

not for you to set us out to be merchandise.

Exploitation *ba jāhiliyah gëmoon ne moom lañ war a def jigéen. . . .*

The exploitation that the *jāhiliyyah* [pre-Islamic Arabs] believed they needed to do to women. . . .

Interestingly, the passage containing the highest frequency of French terms had similar moral connotations and took place in an urban environment, but the object of its criticism was not the West but the speaker's Egyptian neighbor in Cairo whose wife was giving birth the same day the speaker's wife gave birth. The neighbor yelled at God when he found out his wife had had a girl:

> Clinique *bi yaayam* accoucher, *dañu toog. Maa ngi ànd ak benn dëk-kandoor ci* immeuble *bi, man* premier étage *laa nekk, moom mu dëkk* deuxième. . . . *Man* docteur *bi génn, ne ma,* félicitations. . . . *Ba ci tuuti, moom itam, génn ci moom,* salle d'accouchement. . . .
>
> In the clinic where [my son's] mother gave birth, we sat. I went with a neighbor in the building—I lived on the first floor, he lived on the second. . . . The doctor came out and said "congratulations," . . . a little later, he came out to him [the neighbor] too, in the delivery room. . . .

Some of these French loanwords are names for modern things in cities and therefore would normally be in French, yet the passage as a whole is in a contemporary urban register that favors French terms where Wolof terms would normally be used in a religious speech ("gave birth," "congratulations"). His greatest scorn is reserved for colonialism, Orientalism, overly Westernized Senegalese, and liberal critics of Islam who fabricate lies about Islam oppressing women. These passages are full of French terms, even ones whose Wolof equivalents are more commonly used:

> Orientalistes *yii ak* occident *dañuy* blamer *Lislaam, di wax ne Lislaam diine boo xam ne* même *ci* religion *bi dañuy dóor jigéen ñi.*
>
> Orientalists and the West accuse Islam, saying that Islam is a religion [Arabic root] that, even in the religion [that is religious texts, as opposed to custom], they beat women.

A formal speech that sought to avoid French could have easily made a similar point without any of these French words. It is especially interesting that he first uses the universally understood Wolof word for "religion" and then the uncommonly used French word, iconically depicting a Western voice to represent false accusations against Islam.

When reporting a conversation between Baay Ñas and the Catholic first president of Senegal, Léopold Sédar Senghor, the speaker contrasts the latter's voice to that of the former not only by having Senghor use more French words but in ascribing to him drawn-out, French-style guttural *r*'s:

> *[Baay:] "Lenn rekk a la dese: duggal ci Lislaam." Mu ne ko "Sëriñ bi, man am naa diine, te yeen seen diine bi dangay am ay jabarrr yu barrri. Te man benn jabarrr rrrekk doy na ma—Colette—Xanaa ab ak ñaarrri* maîtrrresses." Tu vois*?*
>
> [Baay says:] "You lack only one thing: enter Islam." He [Senghor] said: "*Sëriñ*, I have a rrreligion. And in your rrreligion, you have a lot of wives. As for me, one wife is sufficient—Colette—that is, one with two mistrrresses." [Speaker:] You see?

While not heavy on French words, this passage couples a depiction of Wolof spoken with a heavy French accent—typical among urban non-Wolof with a Francophone education[37]—with the presumably French vice of the "maîtresse," aligning the overly Europeanized former president and perhaps even Christianity with Western moral depravity.

Sometimes a single sentence describes virtuous people or attributes with an Arabic term and vices with a French term:

> *Kuy xas jigéen juy séy, joo xam ne muḥṣnah la, . . . nga ne "Ajaa foo dëkk," mu naan la "lu ma joteek yaw ba nga di laaj fu ma dëkk?" rekk nga jàpp ne kii* femme *bu* vulgaire *la.*
>
> Anyone who puts down a married woman, who is a *lawfully wedded woman* [positive moral connotation], . . . who says 'Ajaa, where do you live?' she replies 'What business do I have with you that you should ask me where I live?' has taken this woman for an indecent woman [negative moral connotation].

Here not only the negative attribute is in French but the accompanying word "woman" too. Perhaps most strikingly, the speaker appropriates the West's terms in passages that describe how Western society devalues, objectifies, and enslaves women:

---

[37] Speaking Wolof with guttural *r*'s is a form of "interference" (Haugen 1956) common among educated Dakar urbanites, especially those of non-Wolof backgrounds. Television advertisements often feature Wolof voices that not only use guttural *r*'s but pronounce Wolof according to French phonology, for example, not distinguishing long and short vowels, emphasizing the last syllable of a phrase, and nasalizing vowels followed by *n* or *m* (for example, pronouncing the Wolof surname Sàmb as if it were French Sambe). The guttural *r* may have entered into Wolof due to the prestige of French, yet speakers whom I have asked about their guttural *r*'s seemed unaware of it.

> Libération *bu dof. Loolu mooy* liberté *bu dof. Moom la tubaab yi indi.*
>
> An insane liberation. That's an insane freedom. That's what the Europeans brought.
>
> *Jigéen, góor dafa jàppoon ne daf fee war a nekk rekk, pur ñu di ci am* satisfaction, *dégg nga,* biologique, *dégg nga,* sèxe *rekk, laysa ʾillā.*
>
> Women, men decided that they should just be there for them to have biological, you see, satisfaction, just sex, *nothing more*.

In the last phrase of this last quote he switches from criticizing Western reductionism using the West's terms to moral condemnation from an Islamic standpoint.

The speaker leans toward Arabic to speak about church-related topics and philosophies, even though these things in Senegal are associated more with European epistemological traditions (a tendency that may be influenced by the fact that he is relying on Arabic texts):

> Philosophe *yi ak rijālu l-kanīsa, mooy nit ñi nga xam ne kilifaay* eglise *bi ak* philosophes *yi, . . .*
>
> Philosophers and *church men,* that is, people who are church leaders and philosophers, . . .
>
> *Mafāhīm yim fi fekkoon yépp,* idéologie-*āt yim fi fekkoon yépp, nga xam ne noonu lañ doon* traîter *jigéen, . . .*
>
> All the *notions* that preceded it [Islam], all the ideologie-*s* [French word, Arabic suffix, used as a gloss for "notions"] that preceded it, which treated women like that, . . .

As the speech progressed, the speaker switched away from this mixed political/academic register into registers more typical of formal religious oratory involving direct quotes from Arabic sources, deep Wolof translations and elaborations, and more conversational Wolof using ordinary French loanwords. Translations of classical Arabic narratives completely dropped French terms, whereas narratives of more recent events took on a more conversational, mixed Wolof. The switch from deep Wolof to conversational Wolof, marked partially by more French terms, shifted attention from a sacred space-time to a modern context shared with the audience.

Thus, in the narrative of Islam's founding, he quoted the Qur'an and other sources in Arabic, translating them into pure Wolof:

> *bam ne ko: ʾiqraʾ—mā ʾanā bi-qāriʾin! la ko wax: jàngal! Mu ne ko duma jàng sëkk! Mu jox ko mu jàng.*
>
> when he said: *Read!—I cannot read!* he [the Angel Jibrīl] told him: Read! He [Muḥammad] told him, I can't read a thing! He gave it to him to read.

In contrast, the follow-up explanation to the classical narrative related it to the modern topic of women's roles in Islam, using several French words that are common in contemporary conversation:

> *Jigéen a njëkk a joxe alalam ci Lislaam: Xaadijatu moo njëkk a* financer *Lislaam . . . ndax* multi-milliardaire *la woon.*
>
> A woman was the first to give her possessions to Islam: Khadījah was the first to finance Islam . . . because she was a multi-billionaire.

He followed the same pattern in the story of Sayyidinā ʿUmar killing his daughter before converting to Islam. He began with pure Wolof and some Arabic during the narrative:

> *Booba tuubagul, mu ngi ci jāhiliyya. . . . Mu ne dafa am doomam bu jigéen, bam am juróom-ñeenti at.*
>
> At that point, he had not yet converted—he was in *pre-Islamic ignorance*. . . . He says that he had a daughter, up until she was *nine years old.*

The use of Wolof to tell the daughter's age clearly marks this as deep Wolof, as conversational Wolof almost always gives ages in French. During the follow-up, he related the story to his audience in the second-person singular, repeating some of the same details but this time using French words:

> *Waaye,* imaginer-*el, am sa doom bam am* neuf ans.
>
> But imagine, you have your child until she is nine years old.

Another story from Islamic history follows the same pattern, telling of a man whose only possession was having memorized verses from the Qurʾān who was told that his dowry would be teaching his wife the Qurʾān. The narrative was entirely in deep Wolof, while the conclusion relating the moral of the story not only shifted to conversational Wolof but appropriated Western discourses on women's education:

> *Kooku,* scolarisation *bu ñuy wax ci* les filles*, xanaa kookoo ci njëkk?*
>
> That man, the schooling that they're talking about for the girls, might we say that he was the first?

This commentary leaps away from the classical Arabic and deep Wolof gloss that preceded it to use not only the French word "filles" (girls) but its French definite article. This hybrid utterance seizes a liberal Western voice to undermine Western attempts to school Muslims about women's oppression.

Conclusion

This speech demonstrates the importance of understanding loanwords and instances of code-switching within a heteroglossic context. In most cases, French terms do not interrupt an otherwise pure Wolof utterance but rather mark the whole utterance as part of a conversational register and contemporary context. Bashiir Ñas's use of such French terms indexed neither hegemonic foreign powers nor the speaker's alignment with them, but rather the speaker's and attendees' shared relationship to contemporary questions. Yet the speaker still distinguished such conversational segments from everyday speech by replacing many French terms with Arabic terms, even though most of these French terms persisted as glosses. Placing the Arabic term first, especially those having positive moral significance, the speaker demoted the French term to the role of gloss, rhetorically anchoring contemporary concerns in traditions of Islamic knowledge and moral authority. Privileging Arabic when describing virtues is a reminder that these concepts are not rooted in Western knowledge regimes even if the speaker needs French terms to communicate with the audience.

In other segments of this speech, an absence of French terms indexed not resistance against Western hegemony but a shift to specialized oratorical registers associated with Islamic knowledge. As we saw earlier, not all Wolof speakers can speak such "deep Wolof," and Islamic specialists' *majlis* education gives them a particularly strong pedagogical grounding in discussing Islamic texts and topics in deep Wolof. As other scholars have noted, Wolof speakers tend to align Wolof as a whole with Islam (Swigart 1994) and even to consider it to be similar to Arabic (Irvine 1989). This association may stem largely from pervasive Wolof discussions on Islamic topics, most notably in the form of oratory. However, it is important to remember that all widely known Taalibe Baay orators can quote extensively from Arabic texts, which they then gloss into deep Wolof and then most often relate to contemporary concerns using a more conversational Wolof. Even lesser known leaders who had not studied Arabic spend considerable energy memorizing Arabic texts and their Wolof gloss in order to be able to speak authoritatively about Islam.

Islamic oratory among Taalibe Baay, and probably among other Senegalese Muslims to the same degree, is therefore deeply heteroglossic through juxtaposing multiple registers. Equally important, speakers invoke multiple registers and voices in hybrid constructions. While many French terms merely mark a conversational register and do not stand out in themselves as foreign, other terms are ideologically marked with either positive or negative connotations. When speakers invoke "Western" values such as freedom and equality, less ideologically marked terms often enter into their discourse as well, suggesting that a Western voice has materialized to be appropriated and undermined in support of an Islamic position. Such hybrid constructions make present globally powerful discourses—for example, in one speaker's words, those of "feminist movements" backed by "big organizations that are international and have a lot of money"[38]—and wrest these powerful discourses away from the West. Projects to bring about liberty and equality, such hybrid discourses insist, can only succeed if situated within Islamic epistemology and morality.

My purpose in focusing on language use in religious oratory has been to draw attention to an important aspect of the larger question of how religious figures perform religious authority in relation to competing yet mutually constitutive institutions and knowledge regimes. These religious authorities seek neither to purify Islam from foreign influences nor to liberalize Islam to fit into a modern, secular world. Rather, they engage in a conversation with multiple knowledge regimes, appropriating liberal discourses while simultaneously resisting the hegemony of liberal institutions and secular assumptions by emphasizing Islam's transcendent

[38] "*Ay* organismes *yu mag ñoo xam ne* international *lañu, bare xaalis*." Abdul Baaqi Dem, Lewna Ñaseen Kaolack, June 12, 2010.

authority. Linguistic hybridity is thus an aspect of a more general hybrid subjectivity informed by an ethos of pragmatic engagement that does not refuse all things "modern," "Western," and "secular." Speakers thus uphold the ultimate legitimacy of Islamic knowledge, authority, and community while acknowledging the practical importance of multiple sources of knowledge.

Bibliography

Agha, Asif. 1998. "Stereotypes and Registers of Honorific Language." *Language in Society* 27, no. 2 (June): 151–93. doi:10.2307/4168831.

Augis, Erin. 2005. "Dakar's Sunnite Women: The Politics of Person." In *L'islam politique au sud du Sahara: Identités, discours et enjeux*, ed. Muriel Gomez-Perez, 309–26. Paris: Karthala.

———. 2009. "Jambaar or Jumbax-out? How Sunnite Women Negotiate Power and Belief in Orthodox Islamic Femininity." In *New Perspectives on Islam in Senegal: Conversion, Migration, Wealth, Power, and Femininity*, ed. Mamadou Diouf and Mara A. Leichtman, 211–33. New York: Palgrave Macmillan.

Babou, Cheikh Anta. 2007. *Fighting the Greater Jihad: Amadu Bamba and the Founding of the Muridiyya of Senegal, 1853–1913*. Athens: Ohio University Press.

Bakhtin, Mikhail. 1981. "Discourse in the Novel." In *The Dialogic Imagination: Four Essays*, ed. Michael Holquist, 259–422. Austin: University of Texas Press.

———. 1986. "The Problem of Speech Genres." In *Speech Genres and Other Essays*, 60–102. Austin: University of Texas Press.

Bourdieu, Pierre. 1991. *Language and Symbolic Power*. Cambridge, MA: Harvard University Press.

Cruise O'Brien, Donal B. 1996. "The Senegalese Exception." *Africa: Journal of the International African Institute* 66, no. 3: 458–64.

Deme, Abdoulaye. 1995. "Les emprunts linguistiques du Wolof à l'Arabe." *Plurilinguismes* 9–10: 15–20.

Diop, Cheikh Anta. 1979. *Nations nègres et culture*. 3rd ed. Vol. 2. Paris: Présence africaine.

Diop, Momar Coumba, ed. 1993. *Senegal: Essays in Statecraft*. Dakar: CODESRIA.

Ferguson, Charles A. 1959. "Diglossia." *Word* 15: 325–40.

Fernandez, James W. 1980. "Edification by Puzzlement." In *Explorations in African Systems of Thought*, ed. Ivan Karp and Charles S. Bird, 44–59. Bloomington: Indiana University Press.

Foucault, Michel. 1984. "Truth and Power." In *The Foucault Reader*, ed. Paul Rabinow, 51–75. New York: Pantheon.

Gumperz, John J. 1977. "The Sociolinguistic Significance of Conversational Code-Switching." *RELC Journal* 8, no. 2 (December 1): 1–34. doi:10.1177/003368827700800201.

Haugen, Einar. 1956. *Bilingualism in the Americas*. Gainesville: American Dialect Society.

Heath, Deborah. 1990. "Spatial Politics and Verbal Performance in Urban Senegal." *Ethnology* 29, no. 3 (July): 209–23.

Hill, Joseph. 2007. "Divine Knowledge and Islamic Authority: Religious Specialization Among Disciples of Baay Ñas." Doctoral dissertation, Yale University.

———. 2010. "'All Women Are Guides': Sufi Leadership and Womanhood Among Taalibe Baay in Senegal." *Journal of Religion in Africa* 40, no. 4: 375–412.

Irvine, Judith T. 1978. "Wolof Noun Classification: The Social Setting of Divergent Change." *Language in Society* 7, no. 1 (April): 37–64. doi:10.2307/4166973.

———. 1989. "When Talk Isn't Cheap: Language and Political Economy." *American Ethnologist* 16, no. 2 (May): 248–67. doi:10.2307/645001.

Johnson, Nancy Kwang. 2004. "Senegalese 'Into Frenchmen'? The French Technology of Nationalism in Senegal." *Nationalism and Ethnic Politics* 10, no. 1 (Spring): 135–58. doi:10.1080/13537110490450809.

Juillard, C., M. L. Moreau, Pape Alioune Ndao, and Ndiassé Thiam. 1994. "Leur wolof dit-il qui ils sont? La perception des appartenances régionales et ethniques au travers du wolof urbain parlé par les adolescents." *Langage et société* 68: 35–62.

Kane, Ousmane, and Leonardo A. Villalón. 1995. "Entre confrérisme, réformisme et islamisme: Les mustarshidin du Sénégal: Analyse et traduction commentée du discours électoral de Moustapha Sy et réponse de Abdou Aziz Sy junior." *Islam et sociétés au sud du Sahara* 9: 119–201.

Klein, Martin A. 1968. *Islam and Imperialism in Senegal: Sine-Saloum, 1847–1914*. Stanford, CA: Stanford University Press.

Labov, William. 1973. "The Linguistic Consequences of Being a Lame." *Language in Society* 2, no. 1 (April): 81–115. doi:10.2307/4166708.

Leichtman, Mara A. 2009. "Revolution, Modernity and (Trans)National Shi'i Islam: Rethinking Religious Conversion in Senegal." *Journal of Religion in Africa* 39 (July): 319–51. doi:10.1163/157006609X461456.

Loimeier, Roman. 1994. "Cheikh Touré: Du reformisme à l'islamisme, un musulman sénégalais dans le siècle." *Islam et sociétés au sud du Sahara* 8: 55–66.

———. 2000. "L'Islam ne se vend plus: The Islamic Reform Movement and the State in Senegal." *Journal of Religion in Africa* 30, no. 2: 168–90.

McLaughlin, Fiona. 1997. "Noun Classification in Wolof: When Affixes Are Not Renewed." *Studies in African Linguistics* 26, no. 1.

———. 2001. "Dakar Wolof and the Configuration of an Urban Identity." *Journal of African Cultural Studies* 14, no. 2: 153–72.

———. 2008. "Senegal: The Emergence of a National Lingua Franca." In *Language and National Identity in Africa*, ed. Adam Simpson, 79–98. Oxford: Oxford University Press.

Myers-Scotton, Carol. 1992. "Comparing Codeswitching and Borrowing." In *Codeswitching*, ed. Carol Eastman, 19–40. Clevedon, UK: Multilingual Matters.

———. 1995. *Social Motivations for Codeswitching: Evidence from Africa.* Oxford: Oxford University Press.

Ndao, Papa Alioune, and Abu Bakri Kébé. 2010. "Langues et médias au Sénégal: Une expérience de normalisation langagière par les journalistes des radios privées: Enjeux et limites." *Glottopol* 14 (January): 17–36.

Ndiaye, Mamadou. 1985. *L'enseignement Arabo-Islamique au Sénégal.* Istanbul: Centre de recherches sur l'histoire, l'art et la culture islamiques.

Ngom, Fallou. 2002. "Linguistic Borrowing as Evidence of the Social History of the Senegalese Speech Community." *International Journal of the Sociology of Language* 158 (October): 37–51. doi:10.1515/ijsl.2002.050.

———. 2003. "The Social Status of Arabic, French, and English in the Senegalese Speech Community." *Language Variation and Change* 15, no. 3: 351–68. doi:10.1017/S0954394503153045.

Robinson, David. 2000. *Paths of Accommodation: Muslim Societies and French Colonial Authorities in Senegal and Mauritania, 1880–1920.* Oxford: James Currey.

Samson, Fabienne. 2005. *Les marabouts de l'islam politique: Le Dahiratoul Moustarchidina wal Moustarchidaty, un mouvement néo-confrérique sénégalais.* Paris: Karthala.

Seesemann, Rüdiger. 2011. *The Divine Flood: Ibrāhīm Niasse and the Roots of a Twentieth-Century Sufi Revival.* Oxford: Oxford University Press.

Sénégal, République du. 1988. *Les principaux résultats provisoires du recensement de la population de l'habitat du Sénégal.* Dakar: République du Sénégal.

———. 2002. *Recensement général de la population et de l'habitat.* Dakar: Agence Nationale de la Statistique et de la Demographie du Sénégal.

Spitulnik, Debra. 1998. "The Language of the City: Town Bemba as Urban Hybridity." *Journal of Linguistic Anthropology* 8, no. 1: 30–59. doi:10.1525/jlin.1998.8.1.30.

Sule, Balaraba B. M., and Priscilla E. Starratt. 1991. "Islamic Leadership Positions for Women in Contemporary Kano Society." In *Hausa Women in the Twentieth Century*, ed. Catherine Coles and Beverly Mack, 29–49. Madison: University of Wisconsin Press.

Swigart, Leigh. 1992a. "Two Codes or One? The Insiders' View and the Description of Codeswitching in Dakar." In *Codeswitching*, ed. Carol Eastman, 83–102. Clevedon, UK: Multilingual Matters.

———. 1992b. "Women and Language Choice in Dakar: A Case of Unconscious Innovation." *Women and Language* 15, no. 1: 11–21.

———. 1994. "Cultural Creolization and Language Use in Post-Colonial Africa: The Case of Senegal." *Africa* 64, no. 2 (June): 175.

———. 2000. "The Limits of Legitimacy: Language Ideology and Shift in Contemporary Senegal." *Journal of Linguistic Anthropology* 10, no. 1: 90–130. doi:10.1525/jlin.2000.10.1.90.

Thiam, Ndiassé. 1990. "L'évolution du wolof véhiculaire en milieu urbain sénégalais: Le contexte dakarois." *Plurilinguismes* 2: 10–37.

———. 1994. "La variation sociolinguistique du code mixte Wolof-français à Dakar: Une première approche." *Langage et société* 68: 11–34.

Villalón, Leonardo A. 1995. *Islam and State Power in Senegal: Disciples and Citizens in Fatick.* Cambridge, UK: Cambridge University Press.

———. 2003. "Generational Changes, Political Stagnation, and the Evolving Dynamics of Religion and Politics in Senegal." *Africa Today* 46, no. 3: 129–47.

Weber, Eugen. 1976. *Peasants into Frenchmen: The Modernization of Rural France, 1870–1914.* Stanford, CA: Stanford University Press.

Woolard, Kathryn A. 1998. "Simultaneity and Bivalency as Strategies in Bilingualism." *Journal of Linguistic Anthropology* 8, no. 1: 3–29. doi: 10.1525/jlin.1998.8.1.3.

ARABIC SCRIPTS IN WEST AFRICAN MANUSCRIPTS: A TENTATIVE CLASSIFICATION FROM THE DE GIRONCOURT COLLECTION

Mauro Nobili
(University of Naples "L'Orientale")
DOI: 10.5192/215409930201105

ABSTRACT

Arabic scripts employed in West African manuscripts have not been fully explored in scholarly literature. The aim of this paper is twofold: to discuss the literature available on this issue and to advance a classification of West African writing styles. This classification is based on the case study of the "de Gironcourt" collection of Arabic manuscripts, gathered in the modern states of Mali, Niger, and Nigeria at the beginning of the twentieth century.

Introduction

A recent statement by Sheila Blair, according to which "the history of Arabic calligraphy in West Africa is a story that is beginning to unfold,"[1] correctly emphasizes that our knowledge about the writing styles employed in West African Arabic manuscripts is unsatisfying.

This paper has two aims. The first one is to offer an overview of some of the literature (published and unpublished) available on West African Arabic scripts. Such an overview identifies two different approaches to the study subject which are significantly affected by theoretical paradigms that shape their unfolding. The first approach subtends research on Muslim

[1] Sheila S. Blair, "Arabic Calligraphy in West Africa," in *The Meanings of Timbuktu*, ed. Shamil Jeppie and Souleymane B. Diagne (Cape Town: Human Sciences Research Council, 2008), 59.

Islamic Africa, VOL. 2, NO. 1, 2011. ISSN 2154-0993. www.islamicafricajournal.org

Africa cultural productions since the mid-eighteenth century and regards the hypothesis that a separation exists between Muslim sub-Saharan Africa and the rest of the Islamic world. The second approach relates to what could be termed a species of "Timbuktucentrism" recently adopted by scholars in the study of the different aspects of the written heritage of Islamic Africa.

The overview expresses the need to engage in a deeper analysis of the Arabic writing styles found in West African manuscripts. The second part of this paper is, thus, devoted to applying this need to the investigation of the case study represented by the manuscripts of the de Gironcourt collection of Arabic manuscripts.[2] In order to address the issues relating to this study, it is useful to recall Murray Last's argument that in West Africa "calligraphy was never the exquisite art form it had become in the Middle East."[3] Save for some remarkable cases, such as the one provided by the calligraphed copies of the Qurʾān from Borno,[4] the region did not generally develop codified calligraphic traditions, nor did it establish schools with prescribed rules, official manuals, etc. Indeed, Blair states that "there is greater deviation from any 'ideal' West African script, and more variety of individual hands."[5] Furthermore, the transmission of writing skills prevalent in northern and sub-Saharan Africa augmented the variability of hands that is connected to the absence of formally codified schools of artists-calligraphers. The system transmission of writing skills in the region is well described by Octave V. Houdas, although in an outdated, condescending tone:

> La déplorable méthode d'enseignement employée aussi bien en Espagne qu'au Maghreb a beaucoup contribué à altérer les types primitives de l'écriture et à en rendre le classement difficile . . . 'Ce n'est pas ainsi, dit l'historien des Berbères [i.e., Ibn Khaldūn], qu'on montre à écrire en

[2] On the de Gironcourt collection, see Mauro Nobili, "'Rediscovering' the de Gironcourt Manuscript Collection," *Annual Review of Islam in Africa* 10 (2008–09): 59–62. A full-scale catalogue of the collection is forthcoming within the *Series Catalogorum* of the Istituto per l'Oriente "C. A. Nallino" (Rome) and CNRS (Paris).

[3] Murray Last, "The Book in the Sokoto Caliphate," in *The Meanings of Timbuktu*, ed. Shamil Jeppie and Souleymane B. Diagne (Cape Town: Human Sciences Research Council, 2008), 151.

[4] Adrian D. H. Bivar, "The Arabic Calligraphy of West Africa," *African Language Review* 7 (1968): 7.

[5] Blair, "Arabic Calligraphy in West Africa," 70.

> Espagne et dans le Maghreb: on n'y apprend pas à former chaque lettre séparément d'après certains principes que le maître enseigne à l'élève; c'est seulement en imitant des mots tout entiers (qui servent de modèles) que l'on apprend à écrire. L'élève tâche d'imiter des mots sous l'inspection du maître, et travaille jusqu'à ce qu'il parvienne à bien faire et que ses doigts aient acquis l'habitude de l'art. On dit alors qu'il sait bien écrire'. Cette façon de procéder n'a pas changé. Au lieu de faire comme en Orient, c'est-à-dire de s'exercer d'abord à tracer les caractères isolés suivant des proportions déterminées, l'étudient maghrébin essaye tout de suite de reproduire dans son ensemble un texte quelconque qu'il a pris comme modèle. Il réussit assez bien à en rendre la physionomie générale, mais il introduit tant de modifications de détail que pas une seule des lettres qu'il a écrit n'est l'image fidèle de celles qu'il s'est attaché à copier.[6]

The lack of a calligraphic level of writing in most West African manuscripts, such as those of the de Gironcourt collection, requires that I avoid the use of the term "calligraphy," which usually refers to a "script that the writer intended to impact the viewer aesthetically."[7] Conversely, I have chosen to employ the terms "script" and "style" because they are exempt from artistic implications and better suit the case of West African manuscripts in Arabic. Script or style are here intended as a sum of different individual hands, sharing some basic features. Such features reveal a certain continuity and homogeneity in their graphic display, which reflect the different traditions of writing adopted by West African scribes.

The choice to focus on the de Gironcourt collection depends on the remarkable characteristics that it presents. This is a unique corpus which allows for a synchronic classification of West African scripts. The vast majority of the manuscripts were realized during a short time span in a wide geographical area including the modern states of Mali, Niger, and Nigeria. Through analyses of the styles displayed by these manuscripts, this paper detects regional variations in a specific time, i.e., the early twentieth century, and provides an in-depth description of the paleographic characteristics of the ʿ*sūqī*ʾ among five identified scripts.

---

6 Octave V. Houdas, "Essai sur l'écriture maghrébine," in *Nouveaux mélanges orientaux* (Paris: Publications de l'École des Langues Orientales Vivantes, 1886), 100–101.
7 Sheila Blair, *Islamic Calligraphy* (Edinburgh: Edinburgh University Press, 2006), xxv.

The Sūdānī *Script*

As of today, there exist no definite labels for the different writing styles used in West Africa. Usually, they are classified under the umbrella term *sūdānī* and its variants, such as the English "Sudanese" or "Sudanic" and the French *soudanais*.

The label *sūdānī* was introduced for the first time at the end of the nineteenth century by Houdas, who used it to identify one of the subtypes of the *maghribī* of poor aesthetic quality.

> L'aspect grossier du soudany . . . le fait aisément reconnaître. Les formes lourdes des lettres sont extrêmement irrégulières; les traits en sont alternativement épais et grêles. Les barres verticales s'élèvent à une grande hauteur, hors de proportion avec la grosseur de l'écriture et la forme des boucles. La pente générale de l'écriture est fortement accentuée et dirigée vers la gauche. Sans cette pente, l'aspect général serait celui d'un grossier coufique tracé par une main mal assurée.[8]

In a paper devoted to the stylistic analysis of a West African Qurʿān published in 1938, Nabia Abbott offers a similar definition of the script employed in this copy of the Islamic holy book. She describes it as "coarse and heavy, being in this respect like the widespread Sudanese variety of the Maghribī script."[9]

The same theoretical framework recurs in a recent study by Blair. She classifies the script used in West Africa as a late subgroup of the *maghribī*, assuming that it developed after the sixteenth century.[10] Blair's remarks have lost much of the condescending attitude of the previous authors, and she states that "the Arabic script typical of West Africa is energetic and lively, a testament of the vigorous tradition of Islam that has flourished there in the last centuries."[11] However, her research still regards the West African script as a sort of degenerated variation of the North African calligraphies that is "sometimes written more hurriedly," being "less

[8] Houdas, "Essai sur l'écriture maghrébine," 104.

[9] Nabia Abbott, "Maghribi Koran Manuscripts of the Seventeenth to Eighteenth Centuries," *American Journal of Semitic Languages and Literatures* 55 (1938): 63.

[10] Blair, "Arabic Calligraphy in West Africa."

[11] Ibid., 72.

polished than the scripts perfected in the East and somewhat rough around the edges."[12]

The literature reported so far seems to share the assumption that the *sūdānī* is somehow primitive and unsophisticated, the expression of a world that is "marginal" to the "center" of the Islamic civilization. The notion rests on the ideological framework informing a hierarchized vision of the Islamic world.[13] This is the theoretical paradigm invoked by Jean Schmitz, based on the "separation of the African Muslims from the wider Islamic world and on the ethnicization of Islam."[14]

In his study of the French perception of Islam in West Africa, Christopher Harrison highlights that the origins of this theory date back to the beginning of the twenteith century and are to be found in the researches of scholars tied to the French administration of African colonies, the likes of Robert Arnaud, Marie-François Joseph Clozel, Maurice Delafosse, Paul Marty, and Jules Brevié.[15]

Since the arrival of Europeans in the region, a belief had surfaced about the supposed superiority of West African Muslims to their non-Muslims neighbors. According to the "social Darwinism" of the period, "Islam, because it had a written culture, was considered midway between barbarism and progress . . . [and] it was seen to be in advance of sub-Saharan societies designated as 'fetishistic.'"[16] A hierarchy was established, based on religious affiliation, that dissolved at the beginning of the twentieth century when the Western perception of Islam in sub-Saharan Africa changed.

Around World War I a shift in the approach of the French towards Islam took place that erased the differences in European engagement with Muslim and non-Muslim societies in Africa. For example, Arnaud stated

[12] Ibid.

[13] For a critique of the notion of a hierarchized Islam, see Alessandro Bausani, "L'Islam: Integrazione o sincretismo religioso?" in *Incontro di religioni in Asia tra il III e il X secolo d. C.*, ed. Lionello Lanciotti (Florence: Olschki, 1984).

[14] Quoted in Constant Hamès, "Les manuscrits arabo-africains: des particularités ?" *Revue des mondes musulmans et de la Méditerranée*, 99–100 [*La tradition manuscrite en écriture arabe*, special issue ed. Geneviève Humbert] (2002): 170.

[15] Christopher Harrison, *French and Islam in West Africa, 1860-1960* (Cambridge, Eng.: Cambridge University Press, 1988).

[16] Jean-Louis Triaud, "Islam in Africa Under French Colonial Rule," in *The History of Islam in Africa*, ed. Nehemia Levtzion and Randall L. Pouwels (Oxford: James Curry, 2000), 171.

that Islam was "still half confused with fetishism,"[17] whereas Clozel added that "the fetishist convert in uttering the ritual formula does not acquire the mentality of the Arab or Berber. . . . The survival of local superstitions, belief in spirits and in an order of ideas, customs and traditions which are often contrary to the rules of the Coran show that the man has made a gesture only."[18] To these declarations Delafosse invoked the argument that "Negroes" were "inherently" hostile to Islam,[19] while Brevié affirmed that it would be a mistake to confuse Islam in the north and in the south of the Sahara.[20] The most comprchensive approach to this matter was, however, contained in Marty's researches, which formulate definitively the theory of *Islam noir*. As stated by Harrison, Marty theorized the existence of "a religion which was distinguished by its *wholesale* adoption of pre-Islamic customs."[21]

As a consequence of this approach, scholars of Islam treated Africa as an "insignificant backwater isolated from the so-called Islamic heartland."[22] For the purpose of this essay, the association of Islam in Africa with primitivism, backwardness, and marginality extends to the study of local Arabic writing styles. Thus, the idea that the *sūdānī* is nothing other than a degenerated reproduction of a more "central" and "sophisticated" archetype must be read in light of this wider disqualification of cultural manifestations of Islam in sub-Saharan Africa.

Furthermore, the reported approach found in Houdas, Abott, and Blair proves to be inadequate from perspectives that pertain to paleography. The immediate and exclusive derivation of West African scripts from the *maghribī*, or their classification as a subgroup of North African calligraphic styles, has been accepted as a given fact in the literature. However, other studies, to which unfortunately only insufficient attention has been paid, question the theory of a direct derivation of the Sudanese styles from a North African antecedent. Nico van den Boogert, for example, denies that the *sūdānī* descends directly from the *maghribī*.[23] Adrian Brock-

[17] Harrison, *French and Islam*, 96.
[18] Ibid., 99.
[19] Ibid., 146.
[20] Ibid., 147.
[21] Ibid., 203 (my italics).
[22] Scott S. Reese, "Islam in Africa: Challenging the Perceived Wisdom," in *The Transmission of Learning in Islamic Africa*, ed. Scott R. Reese (Leiden: Brill, 2004), 2.
[23] Nico van den Boogert, "Some Notes on Maghribi Script," *Manuscripts of the Middle East* 4 (1987): 31.

ett stresses the idea that the origin of West African scripts is to be found in the ancient Western Kufic,[24] while Constant Hamès emphasizes that the influence of Egypt has been considerable in the development of West African styles.[25] In the same way, Adrian D. H. Bivar posits that the ancient Kufic constitutes the main relevant model in the formation of West African scripts and that Egyptian influences are an important element in their development, mentioning also the impact that cursive Eastern Sudanese models have had on them.[26]

Moreover, bringing all the West African styles under a single label, the *sūdānī*, leads us to underestimate the huge differences that characterize the various scripts developed in the region. A brief look at any collection of manuscripts produced south of the Sahara clearly shows that some of these styles have little in common in terms of the stroke, the shape of the letters, or the general appearance of handwritten pages.[27] Recalling Hamès' recent statement in relation to some West African copies of the Qurʾān will aid in further stressing this point. Commenting on the scripts displayed in these manuscripts, Hamès observes that the only shared calligraphic characteristics are the *fāʾ* written with a single dot under the letter and the *qāf* with one dot above the letter in their initial and medial position, as well as the unpointed final *fāʾ*, *qāf*, and *nūn*.[28] He also adds that relevant divergences distinguish the different scripts employed in the manuscripts he analyzes.[29]

To the best of my knowledge, the above-mentioned Bivar, in a late 1960s paper devoted to the development of northern Nigerian styles across the centuries, is the first scholar who has attempted to single out and describe different subgroups within the broader category of the *sūdānī*.[30]

---

24 Adrian Brockett, "Aspects of the Physical Transmission of the Qurʾān in 19th-Century Sudan: Script, Decoration, Binding and Paper," *Manuscripts of the Middle East* 2 (1987): 45.

25 Hamès, "Les manuscrits arabo-africains," 177.

26 Bivar, "The Arabic Calligraphy of West Africa," 3–15.

27 The same observation is prompted by looking at the pictures of manuscripts recently published by John O. Hunwick and Alida Boye Hunwick, *The Hidden Treasures of Timbuktu* (London: Thames and Hudson, 2008).

28 Constant Hamès, "Corans africains manuscripts: Vers une typologie," in *Le temps des Oulemas: Les manuscripts africains comme sources historique,* ed. Seyni Moumouni and Viera Pawlikova-Vilhanova (Niamey: Université Abdou Moumouni de Niamey et Union Académique Internationale, 2009), 47.

29 Ibid., 54

30 Bivar, "The Arabic Calligraphy of West Africa."

His research, however, focuses exclusively on northern Nigeria and relies solely on manuscripts produced in this region, as clearly stated by the author.[31] As a consequence of such a choice, Bivar's classification, though stimulating, can hardly be applied to other sub-Saharan regions. In spite of this premise and of Blair's critique,[32] Bivar's hypothesis offers some useful analytical suggestions that I employ in the following classification.

West African Scripts in the Classification of Local Scholars

Recently, the study of West African writing styles has been undertaken by local scholars who propose a classification that offers an insight into the local perception of the styles developed in sub-Saharan Africa. The development of this classification was integral to the cataloguing project of the manuscripts hosted at the Institute des Hautes Études et de Recherche Islamique Ahmed Baba (IHERIAB), formerly the Centre de Documentation et de Recherches Historiques Ahmad Baba (CEDRAB), which was launched in the mid-1990s by the al-Furqan Islamic Heritage Foundation and was eventually adopted by other West African scholars working on other collections of manuscripts.

Beside Oriental and North African scripts, this classification identifies in the manuscripts of the sub-Saharan region three local styles: *saharienne/ ṣaḥrāwī*, *sūdānī/sudanaise*, and *sūqi*.

Regarding the *saḥrāwī*, Seyni Moumouni argues that it is the most widespread script of sub-Saharan Africa.[33] He suggests that

> l'écriture dite "saharienne" est la plus courante à Tombouctou. Elle est l'écriture de tous les jours, très cursive, tracée au petit calame souple; elle est ronde pour s'écrire plus vite et étroite pour économiser le papier.[34]

---

[31] Ibid., 4.

[32] Ibid., 66.

[33] Seyni Moumouni, "Les manuscrits africains en écriture arabe et Ajami: Essai de codicologie et de paléographie," in *Patrimoine et sources historiques en Afrique*, ed. Ibrahima Thioub (Dakar: Université Cheikh Anta Diop de Dakar et Union Académique Internationale, 2007), 55.

[34] M. Mohammed Galla Dicko et al., "Trèsors écrits du centre Ahmed Baba de Tombouctou," in *Les bibliothèques du désert: Recherches et études sur un millénaire d'écrits,* ed. Attilio Gaudio (Paris: Harmattan, 2002), 222.

In an interesting, unpublished paper on West African manuscripts, the Timbuktu calligrapher Maḥmūd Muḥammad Dadab al-Tinbuktī al-Arawānī, known as Ḥammū, adds a further description of this calligraphic style.[35] He presents the *ṣaḥrāwī* as the script of the Songhay and of the people of the desert, west of Timbuktu.[36] The author also shortly presents some of its paleographic peculiarities.[37]

As for the *sūqī*, we learn from M. Mohammed Galla Dicko et al. that it is the style of the Tuareg: "sharp and precise, the script is very regular and narrow, the curves are sometimes indented."[38]

Finally, notwithstanding the introduction of new, more precise definitions of local scripts, the label *soudanaise/sūdānī* resurfaces:

> Le style *sudanî* fut probablement créé à Tombouctou mais se répandit dans toute la région subsaharienne, descendant au sud jusqu'au Nigeria. C'est l'écriture préférée des Haoussas, les lignes sont épaisses, les lettres denses donnent une écriture massive souvent ornée de motifs que l'on retrouve dans les broderies des mêmes régions . . .[39]

While in this quotation the *sūdānī* is still used as an all-encompassing label, Ḥāmmū correctly suggests that more than a specific script, the *sūdānī* is a generic label referring to styles that are not classifiable according to the other categories. He writes that the *sūdānī* includes different scripts used by the Fulani, the Songhay,[40] the Wolof, and the Hausa, the latter calligraphy also called *barnāwī*.[41] Seyni Moumouni remarks that among the Hausa, a specific script has developed through time.[42]

Unfortunately, a 2008 paper by Sidi Mohammed Ould Youbba is the

[35] Maḥmūd Muḥammad Dadab al-Arawānī al-Tinbuktī (Ḥammū), "Al-Kashf ʿan al-makhṭūṭāt al-ʿarabiyya wa-al-maktūba bil-ḥarf al-ʿarabī fī minṭaqat al-Sāḥil al-Ifrīqī." I thank the author for sharing this unpublished paper.

[36] Ibid., 16.

[37] Ibid., 16–17.

[38] Dicko et al., "Trèsors écrits," 222 (translation from the French mine).

[39] Ibid., 222.

[40] Ḥammū is ambiguous on the calligraphy employed by the Songhay. While they are described as users of the *ṣaḥrāwī*, the Songhay are also credited with making use of a specific typology of the *sūdānī*.

[41] Ḥammū, "Al-Kashf," 16.

[42] S. Moumouni, "Les manuscrits africains," 55, n. 1.

only available study presenting some pictures of manuscripts whose calligraphies are respectively categorized as *maghribī*, *saḥrāwī*, *sūdānī*, and *sūqī*.[43] Photographs are, in fact, generally missing from classificatory studies, although they would represent an invaluable resource for scholars who have not had the opportunity to work daily on the actual manuscripts. Ould Youbba's study is an exception, although he does not provide any classificatory criteria of the photographed styles.

The classification developed by West African scholars has also been recently adopted by John O. Hunwick and Alida Boye.[44] Unfortunately, these scholars do not go in depth with their analysis of calligraphic styles, especially considering that they seem to work with important sources that most researchers would find difficult to access.[45] As for the styles, they report:

> Saharian (*ṣaḥrāwī*) calligraphy is used by the Moors and their students. This is characterized by its angularity, with unusual height in certain letters as well as exaggerated lengthening of others.
>
> *Sūqī* or Sanhajan calligraphy, used by Berber scholars. This is a distinctive style associated with the scholars of the Kel al-Suq.
>
> Sudanese (*sūdānī*), possibly originating from Maghrebian calligraphy with some influence from ancient Kufic. Used by the Songhay, Fulani,

---

43 Sidi Mohammed Ould Youbba, "The Ahmed Baba Institute of Advanced Islamic Studies and Research," in *The Meanings of Timbuktu*, ed. Shamil Jeppie and Souleymane B. Diagne (Cape Town: Human Sciences Research Council, 2008), 294–95.

44 Hunwick and Boye, *The Hidden Treasures*, 98–99.

45 They mention the following publications, which I have not been able to collect for the present paper: (a) Abdel Kader Haïdara, "Bibliothèque Mamma Haïdara de Tombouctou," in *Chemins du Savoir: Les manuscrits arabes et a'jami dans la région soudano-sahélienne. Colloque International 13–17 juin 2005, Rabat* (Rabat: Institut des Études Africaines, 2006); (b) Mohamed Maghraoui, *Guide de l'exposition sur les manuscrits de Tombouctou: Patrimoine Partagé, Rabat 13–17 juin 2005. Bibliothèque Nationale du Royaume du Maroc* (Rabat: Institut des Études Africaines, 2005); (c) Bruno Marty, "Histoire de l'écriture," in *Les trésors manuscrits de la Méditerranée*, ed. Abdelhamid Arab et al. (Dijon: Éditions Faton, 2005). They affirm that their analysis of West African writing styles has been carried out in collaboration with Philippe Roisse, Centre de Documentation et de Recherches Arabes Chrétiennes (CEDRAC), University of St. Joseph, Beirut, and Mohamed Maghraoui, Université Mohamed V–Agdal, Rabat, for providing clarifications to this description of styles of calligraphy used in West Africa (Hunwick and Boye, *The Hidden Treasures*, 153, notes to chapter 2, n. 25).

> Tukulor, Soninke, Wolof and Hausa, this is characterized by thick letters.[46]

I must underline here that Hunwick and Boye's description of the *ṣaḥrāwī* differs substantially from the above-mentioned research by West African scholars. Hunwick and Boye describe the calligraphy as the script of the "Moors," probably referring to the *biḍān* inhabitants of the desert and the Sahel. This seems to imply that *sūdānī* scholars are not included among the users of the *ṣaḥrāwī*. Furthermore, the angularity that they describe as the main characteristic of the script is unmatched by paleographic evidence, as will be discussed in the following paragraph. Moreover, it is very unfortunate that the authors, whose book includes high-quality pictures of wonderful manuscripts, never match script labels to images, depriving scholars of a very useful tool of comparative analysis.

This overview evidences that local scholars have mainly focused on the *ṣaḥrāwī* and *sūqī* scripts that are widespread among the scribes of the Timbuktu region. On the other hand, less attention has been paid to different styles peculiar to other West African regions, classified under the resurging *sūdānī* label which groups scripts whose features are unfamiliar to Timbuktu's cultural milieu. It could be inferred, then, that the writing culture of Timbuktu has emerged as the dominant analytical paradigm for scholars working with West African manuscripts and that a certain "Timbuktucentrism" prevails in current researches on the written heritage of Islamic Africa.

To sum up my review of the state of the art of studies on West African scripts, it is worth quoting again Hunwick and Boye's remark that "much work remains to be done in studying and classifying these different scripts."[47] Embracing this suggestion, the following paragraphs discuss the writing styles found in the de Gironcourt collection of West African manuscripts.

West African Scripts in the de Gironcourt Collection

The de Gironcourt collection of Arabic manuscripts was donated to the library of the Institut de France at the return of the French *ingénieur-agronome* Georges de Gironcourt (1878–1960) to Paris at the end of 1912.

[46] Hunwick and Boye, *The Hidden Treasures*, 99.

[47] Ibid., 98.

During an archeological mission to West Africa financed by the Ministry of Colonies, the Ministry of Public Instruction, and the Academy of Inscriptions and Belles Lettres, de Gironcourt collected 812 *estampages* of inscriptions in both Arabic and Tifinagh alphabet, as well as a number of manuscripts in Arabic and French.[48] Most of the documents in the collection are "copies" of manuscripts owned by local marabouts[49] that were made for de Gironcourt by local scribes during his journey. There are also four manuscripts dating back to an older epoch, the eighteenth and nineteenth centuries. Furthermore, the collection hosts several documents that are particularly interesting. These documents consist of "notes" about local traditions, historical events, genealogies, and obituaries that local scholars dictated to copyists by heart or wrote themselves at de Gironcourt's request.

Due to the circumstances of their writing, the manuscripts offer a particularly useful perspective on West African calligraphies. Leaving aside the older documents, all the manuscripts originated from a wide area of West Africa and are coeval. The dates of copying of the manuscripts were carefully recorded by the French explorer in a *fiche signalétique* preceding every manuscript. All documents were copied during the mission of de Gironcourt from November 1, 1911 to August 15, 1912. The *fiche signalétique* also indicates the location where the French explorer had his copy made and reports notes on the copyist/s. The manuscripts come from a region extending from Masina, in central Mali, to the border between the modern states of Niger and Nigeria and the Saharan mountains of the Adrar-des-Ifoghas and were copied by scribes of many ethnic and tribal affiliations. Due to the characteristic coeval nature of the manuscripts and the distributed geographical origin, the collection brings together a unique set of documents that well suit a comparative study of West African scripts.

However, even among the scripts identified in the de Gironcourt collection, the manuscripts may show hands that present slightly different

---

[48] In spite of the common West African practice to write local "Islamic" languages in the Arabic alphabet (*ʿAjamī*), especially by the Fulfulde, Songhay, Kanuri, and Hausa, the de Gironcourt manuscripts show no trace of the use of *ʿAjamī* but its mention in a few notes.

[49] My use of the outdated term "marabout" reproduces de Gironcourt's own colonial French terminology. The term "includes not only those most generally referred as *ʿulamāʾ*—the *qāḍī*s and other respected jurisprudents and teachers—but *imām*s, *khatīb*s, sufis, ascetics, pietists and in general all those who may be described as 'holymen' "(John O. Hunwick, "Secular Power and Religious Authority in Islam: The Case of Songhay," *Journal of African History* 37, no. 2 [1996]: 176).

features. Along with the general consideration about the transmission of writing skills in West Africa contained in the introduction to this paper, it must be noted that the quality of the manuscripts collected by de Gironcourt is especially poor. Hunwick and Hasan I. Gwarzo state that "one might conclude that in many cases he [de Gironcourt] was in fact duped by unscrupulous persons who no doubt brought him any scrap of Arabic writing they could find in order to receive some reward."[50] Although their opinion could be debated, it is certainly true that, in some cases, the quality of the scripts reflects the work of unprofessional scribes. It must also be underlined that the copies were made hastily in a short time at the request of de Gironcourt, during his brief stop in a particular town or village. Thus, it comes as no surprise that the de Gironcourt manuscripts display hands that sometimes may vary among themselves, making this classifying effort very difficult.

Notwithstanding the differences among the scripts displayed in the de Gironcourt collection, all the manuscripts are written in more or less cursive scripts that, except for a few cases, share some basic characteristics:

- The letters *fāʾ* and *qāf* are pointed in the Western fashion, that is, with one point under the *fāʾ* and one point over the *qāf*;
- Final *fāʾ*, *qāf,* and *nūn* are pointless;
- Final *nūn*, *sīn*, *shīn*, *ṣād,* and *ḍād* usually have an exaggerated curved trait that runs under the following word;
- *Ṣād* and *ḍād* are always realized without the "tooth";
- The *bāʾ* in the *basmala* is usually as high as an *alif* or *lām* and sometimes higher;
- The lower tail of an isolated or final *mīm* is not straight;
- The stroke of a connected *alif* is often prolonged under the baseline;
- Final *yāʾ* and *alif maqsūra* may curve towards the right.

One may be tempted to use these shared peculiarities as proof to describe an overall sub-Saharan tradition justifying the existence of a *sūdānī* label. However, all these characteristics are peculiar not only to West African calligraphies, but, as shown in the descriptive paper on *maghrībī* by

[50] John O. Hunwick and Hasan I. Gwarzo, "Another Look at the de Gironcourt Papers," *Research Bulletin: Centre of Arabic Documentation* 3, no. 2 (1967): 76.

Boogert,[51] recur in all Western Arabic calligraphies. Therefore, they do not seem to constitute sufficient evidence for the use of the label *sūdānī*.

Let us now take a direct look at the de Gironcourt manuscripts and propose a tentative classification of the calligraphies represented in the manuscripts.[52] For each of these styles, I describe some specific features that characterize it and, at the end of the paper, present one or more pictures for each script.

Maghribī—Some de Gironcourt manuscripts are realized in *maghribī* even if they may present some influences of West African styles. These manuscripts were made by the Kunta shaykh Muḥammad *al-saghīr* bin ʿUmar, known as Bāy (d. after 1920); by some scholars related to him; and by one chief of Bida, a settlement not far from Gao, that claims sharifian descent. It is worth noting that most of the scribes employing the *maghrībī* were Kunta, suggesting that their strong cultural and commercial links with North Africa may have influenced the adoption of this style.

Ṣaḥrāwī (figure 1)—In Timbuktu de Gironcourt collected a group of manuscripts whose scripts can clearly be ascribed to a coherent style. These manuscripts were produced by two different scribes: "Lehabib bin Zeini"[53] and al-Suyūṭī bin Muḥammad.

The first scholar was, following de Gironcourt's notes, a sharif from Walata who lived in Timbuktu. He was a professional copyist in Timbuktu during the end of the nineteenth century and the beginning of the twentieth century and made for the famous French journalist Felix Dubois a copy of the *Tarīkh al-Sūdān* which has been used by Houdas in his edition of this text.[54]

The second copyist is the imam al-Suyūṭī bin Muḥammad, a well-known early twentieth-century Timbuktu scholar. Born around 1865,

[51] Van den Boogert, "Some Notes on Maghribi Script."

[52] The forthcoming catalogue of the de Gironcourt collection employs the classification of writing styles advanced by this paper. Each manuscript is accompanied by a description note that includes, among other information, a reference picture and the annotation of the script style.

[53] In the case of copyists whose names are not known in their Arabic form, I employ de Gironcourt's spelling in between quotation marks.

[54] Octave V. Houdas, trans., *Tarikh Es-Soudan* (Paris: Adrien-Maissoneuve, 1964).

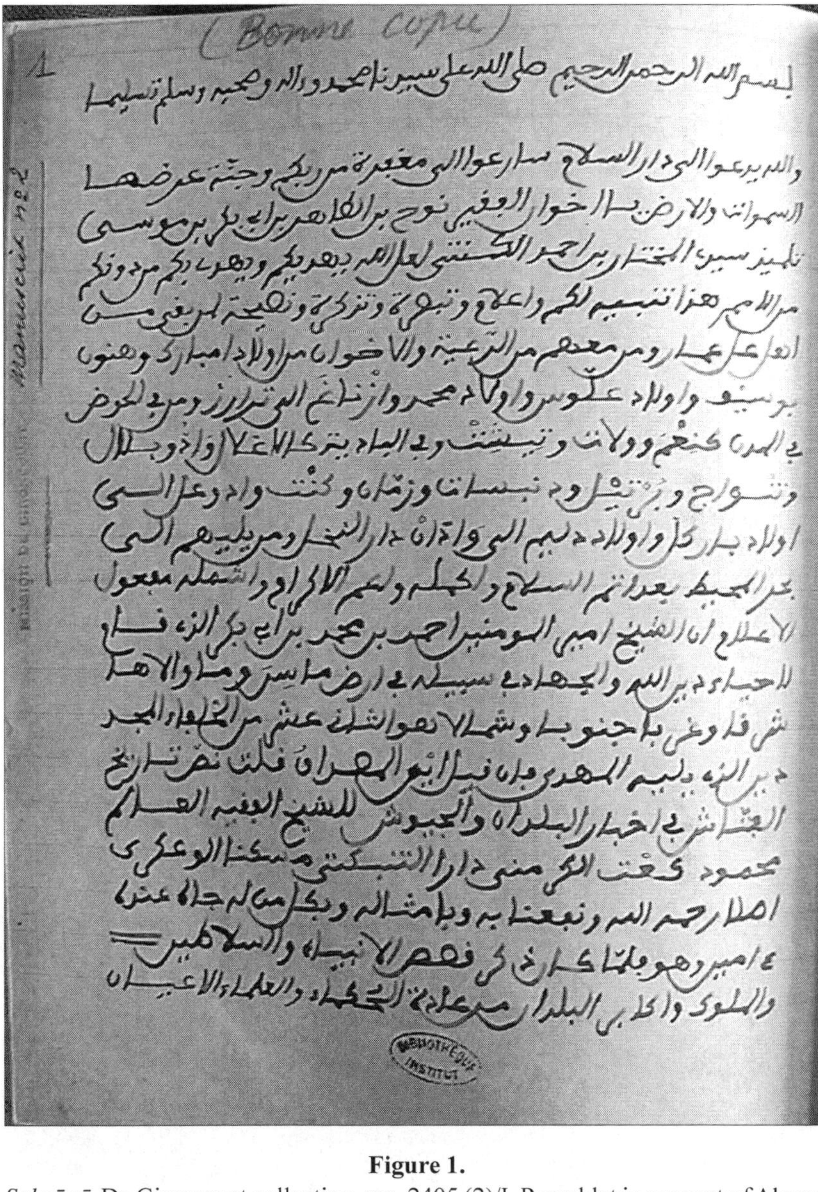

(Bonne copie)

بسم الله الرحمن الرحيم صلى الله على سيدنا محمد وآله وصحبه وسلم تسليما

والله يدعوا الى دار السلام سارعوا الى مغفرة من ربكم وجنة عرضها السموات والارض

Figure 1.

Ṣaḥrāwī. De Gironcourt collection, ms. 2405 (2)/I. Pamphlet in support of Aḥamd bin Muḥammad, caliph of Masina (d. 1845). Copied by al-Suyūṭī b. Muḥammad in Timbuktu (1911). Courtesy of Bibliothèque de l'Institut, Paris.

al-Suyūṭī taught Islamic law at the French *medersa* of Timbuktu.[55] His high scholarly reputation is confirmed by the role of proofreader that he performed for some of the manuscripts collected by de Gironcourt.

The manuscripts made by these two copyists present a high degree of homogeneity. Indeed, both copyists appear to be specialized scholars and thus fully capable of following a specific style, of reproducing a fixed set of peculiarities, and of sticking to an "ideal" script. On the basis of a comparison with the photographic exemplar provided by Ould Youbba[56] and the description of Ḥāmmū,[57] their style emerges as an example of the *saḥrāwī*. The fact that the copyists come from the cultural milieu of Timbuktu confirms the suggestion of local scholars that this city was one of the centers where the *ṣaḥrāwī* script was employed.

The *ṣaḥrāwī* is a cursive script characterized by a thick stroke, as if it were drawn with a blunt pen. Sometimes, the stroke is so thick that it is almost impossible to distinguish the letters *bāʾ*, *tāʾ*, *thāʾ*, *fāʾ*, *qāf*, *mīm*, *nūn*, and *yāʾ* in their medial position except for their diacritical points. Also, on some occasions, it is possible that the thickness of the stroke fills in the empty spaces inside the letters *fāʾ*, *qāf*, *mīm*, *hāʾ*, *wāw*, and medial *ʿayn* and *ghayn*. The script bends to the right and the words are often written on a slope. Furthermore, the *ṣaḥrāwī* does not feature any perpendicular junctions between horizontal and vertical traits.[58] Among the characteristic features of this style, it can be noted that the *rāʾ* and *zāʾ* are often hooked. The *dāl* and *dhāl* are slightly open, lacking the upper trait and descending under the baseline. Thus, they become indistinguishable from regular *rāʾ* and *zāʾ*.

The *ṣaḥrāwī* resembles the *jihādī* introduced by Bivar,[59] to the point that it is treated in this paper as the same style. However, the conclusion suggests that the label *ṣaḥrāwī* is to be preferred to *jihādī*. In his research, Bivar stresses the strong influence of the *maghribī* script, which he calls "Andalusian," on the development of the *jihādī/ṣaḥrāwī,* and this influence is fully confirmed by the remarkable similarities between *jihādī/ṣaḥrāwī* and several cursive scripts employed in the North African (both

---

[55] William Seabrook, *The White Monk of Timbuktu* (New York: Harcourt Brace, 1934), 190. On this scholar, see Paul Marty, *Étude sur l'Islam et sur les tribus du Soudan: Tome II: La région de Tombouctou (Islam songhay), Dienné, le Macina et dépendances (Islam peul)* (Paris: Éditions Ernest Leroux, 1920), 15–17.

[56] Youbba, "The Ahmed Baba Institute," 295.

[57] Ḥammū, "Al-Kashf," 16.

[58] This specific feature contradicts Hunwick and Boye's consideration about the supposed angularity of *ṣaḥrāwī* discussed above.

[59] Bivar, "The Arabic Calligraphy of West Africa," plate V.

from Maghreb and Egypt) and the Andalusian manuscripts presented by Georges Vajda in his *Album de Paléographie Arabe.*[60]

Central Sudanic cursive hands (figures 2–3)—In Sinder[61] and Say, in the modern state of Niger, de Gironcourt collected a number of manuscripts belonging to the same calligraphic tradition but showing relatively dissimilar hands. These manuscripts were copied by the disciples of the Songhay marabout Yūsuf bin al-Khalīl. The latter was supervisor and proofreader at a sort of school, where disciples acted as copyists, often working together on the same manuscript. These manuscripts display beautiful multicolor decorations, resembling the decorated manuscripts that were produced in northern Nigeria until the twentieth century. They present the use of two or three colors (red, yellow, and green), besides the black of the main body of the text, as described by Last.[62] However, in spite of a recognizable carefulness in the aesthetic execution, the copyists' hands still display some differences among themselves.

Within al-Khalīl's school, one scribe in particular attracted my attention due to his hand, which is very peculiar, polished, and decorative. The scribe's name is "Haruna Alfaga," and de Gironcourt notes that he was a Songhay marabout.

The hands of Yūsuf al-Khalīl's disciples show some similarities with the scripts found in the manuscripts that de Gironcourt collected in Kandadji, not far from Ansongo. Such hands differ markedly from the other calligraphies described in this paper and are close to what Bivar defines as "current Nigeran hands."[63] An example of a current Nigerian hand is represented in the de Gironcourt collection by the manuscripts 2416 (222–223)/I and 2416 (222–223)/II. These manuscripts, whose copyist/s is/are not mentioned, were obtained in Badjibo, Nigeria, but they were probably made in Busa by a marabout of the king's court.[64]

As regards this style, Bivar's choice of label name remains unsatisfactory. The scholar's research refers only to cursive hands employed in Nigeria, whereas features characterizing these hands appear to be spread

[60] Georges Vajda, *Album de paléographie arabe* (Paris: Adrien-Maisonneuve, 1958).

[61] This town is located on the river Niger and it is not to be confused with the more famous city of Zinder.

[62] Last, "The Book in the Sokoto Caliphate," 152.

[63] Bivar, "The Arabic Calligraphy of West Africa."

[64] Paulo F. de Moraes Farias, "A Letter From Ki-Toro Mahamman Gaani, King of Busa (Borgu, Northern Nigeria) about the 'Kisra' Stories of Origin (*c.* 1910)," *Sudanic Africa* 3 (1992): 109–132. The paper includes good-quality pictures of the manuscripts.

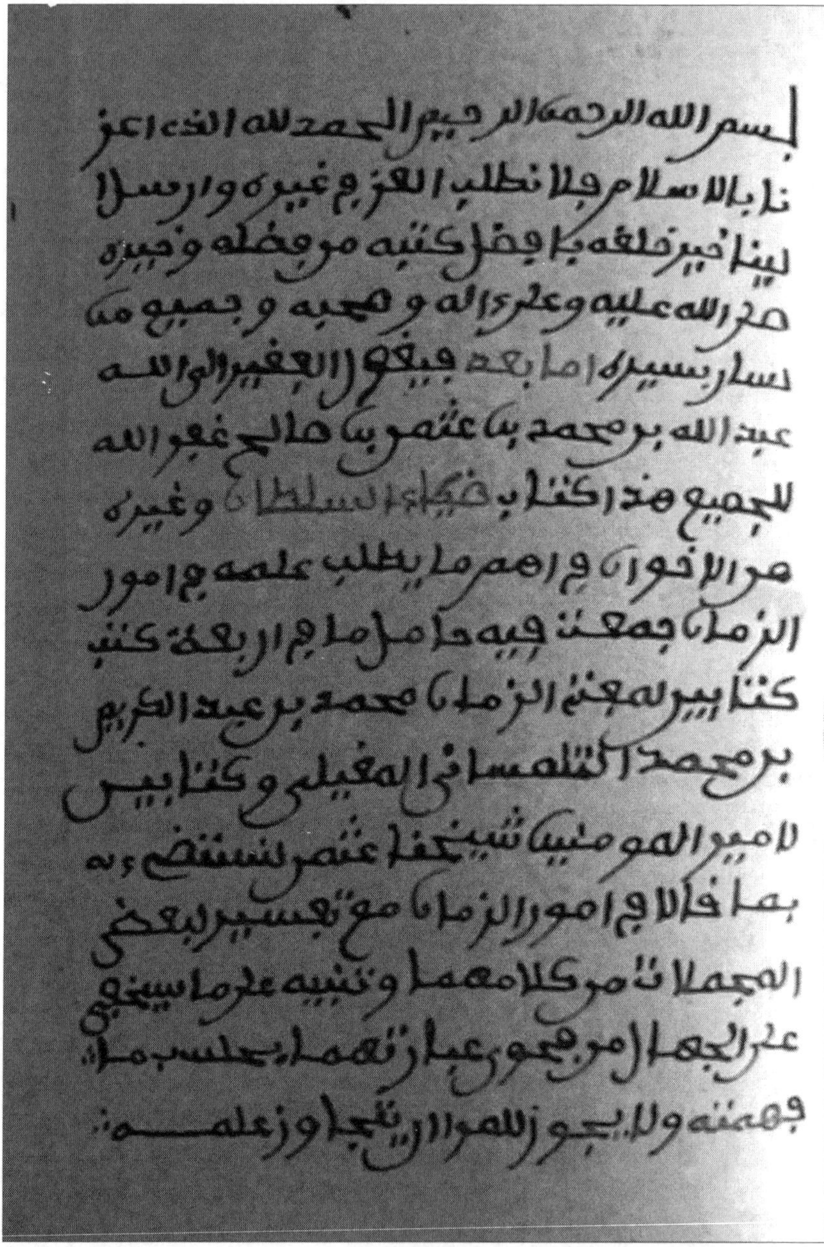
بسم الله الرحمن الرحيم الحمد لله الذي أعز
نا بالإسلام فلا نطلب العز في غيره وأرسل إ
لينا خير خلقه بأفضل كتبه من فضله وخيره
صلى الله عليه وعلى آله وصحبه وجميع من
سار بسيره أما بعد فيقول العبد الفقير إلى الله
عبد الله بن محمد بن عثمن بن صالح غفر الله
للجميع هذا كتاب ضياء السلطان وغيره
من الإخوان في أهم ما يطلب علمه في أمور
الزمان جمعت فيه حاصل ما في أربعة كتب
كتاب تبيين لمعنى الزمان لمحمد بن عبد الكريم
بن محمد التلمساني المغيلي وكتاب تبيين
لأمير المؤمنين شيخنا عثمن لنستفيد به
بما خالف في أمور الزمان مع تفسير لبعض
المجملات من كلامهما وتنبيه على ما ينبغي
على الجهال من فهم عبارتهما بحسب ما
فهمته ولا يجوز للمرء أن يتجاوز علمه

Figure 2.
Example of Central Sudanic hand. De Gironcourt collection, ms. 2415 (205). *Ḍiyā' al-sulṭān* by ʿAbd Allāh bin Fūdī. Copied by some of the disciples of Yūsuf bin al-Khalīl in Sinder (1912). Courtesy of Bibliothèque de l'Institut, Paris.

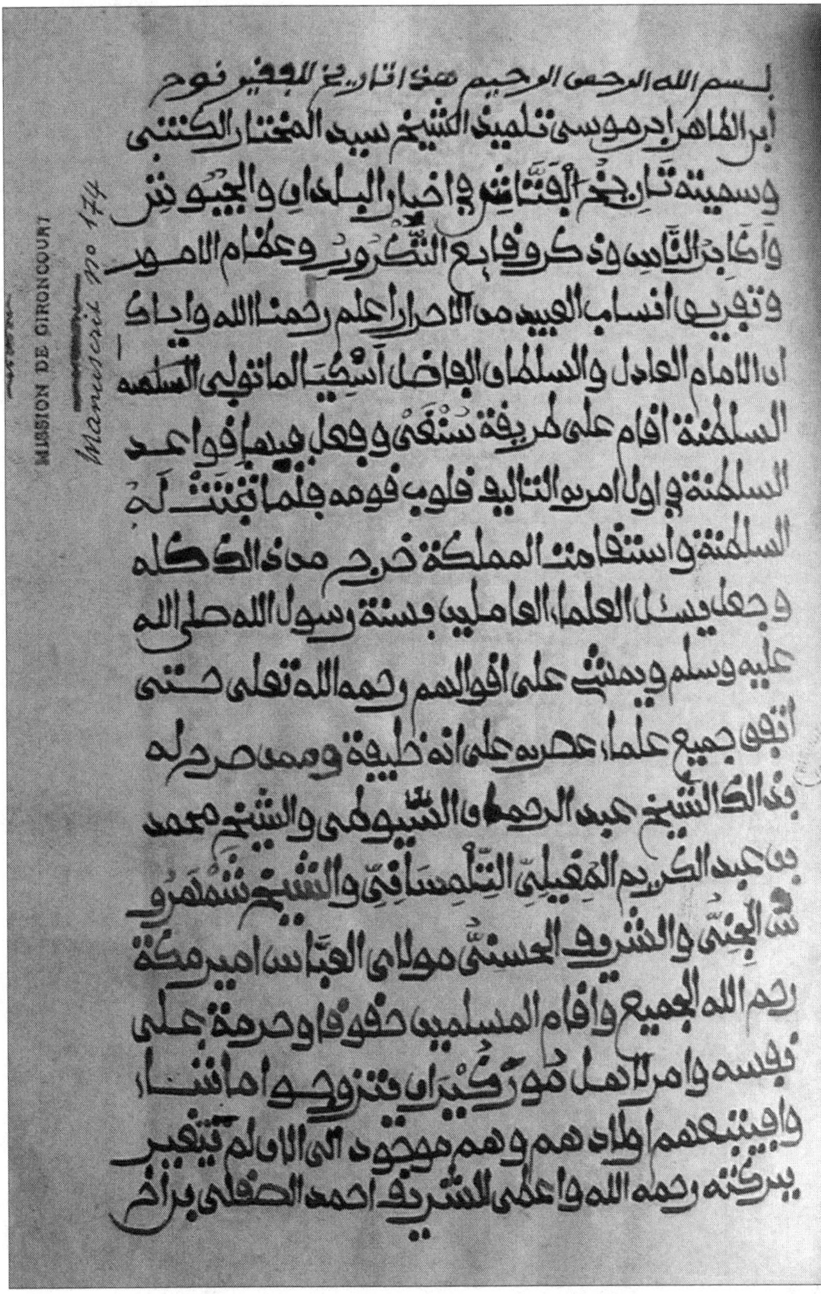

Figure 3.
Example of a beautiful Central Sudanic hand. De Gironcourt collection, ms. 2410 (174). Pamphlet in support of Aḥamd bin Muḥammad, caliph of Masina (d. 1845). Copied by "Haruna Alfaga," disciple of Yūsuf bin al-Khalīl, in Sinder (1912). Courtesy of Bibliothèque de l'Institut, Paris.

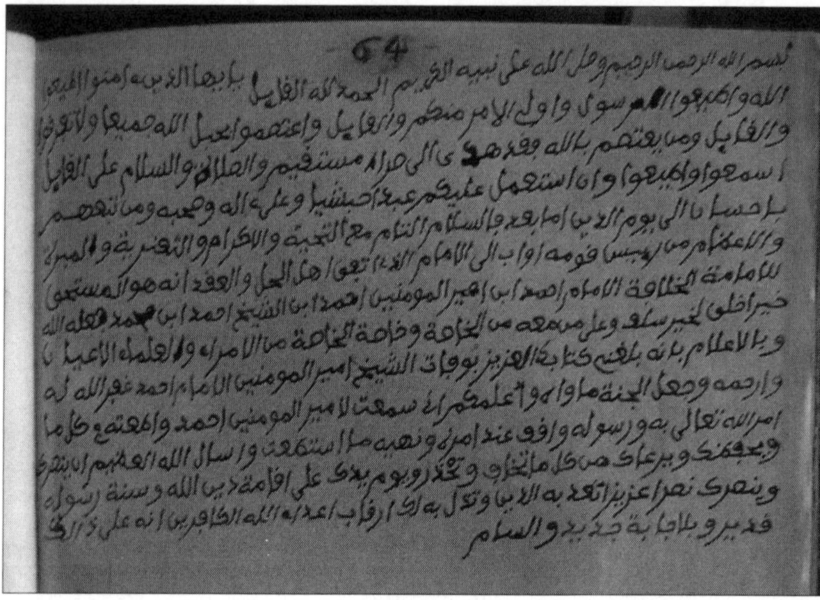

Figure 4.

Example of Masina hand. De Gironcourt collection, ms. 2406 (64). Letter of Awāb, chief of the Kel Tadamakkat, to Aḥmad bin Aḥmad (d. 1862), last caliph of Masina. Copied by a Masina (1911). Courtesy of Bibliothèque de l'Institut, Paris.

in a wider region including, besides Niger and Nigeria, also Ghana[65] and Chad.[66] These hands may be a less polished and decorative, cursive version of the Kufic hands traditionally employed in the Bornu-made copies of the Qur'ān, which Bivar calls "Bornu court hand."[67] My choice to address them collectively as "Central Sudanic cursive hands" is a way to bring together hands that share common features which, however, are yet to be satisfactorily described.

Masina hands (figure 4)—As regards scripts, the most puzzling region visited by de Gironcourt is Masina. The manuscripts were copied by many different Fulbe copyists in four towns of Masina: Djenné, Dia, Sossobé,

[65] My thanks go to Dr. Andrea Brigaglia for sharing with me his research on the manuscripts of the University of Ghana Arabic Manuscript Collection at the Herskovits Library, Northwestern University.

[66] See the Qur'ān from Chad described in Hamès, "Corans africains manuscripts."

[67] Bivar, "The Arabic Calligraphy of West Africa," 10.

and Ténenkou. Their hands do not fit into any of the labels proposed in the literature on the topic, and most scholars would probably describe them simply, and collectively, as *sūdānī*.

The hands employed in these documents differ markedly among themselves and it is not possible, at the moment, to propose a detailed description of this style and provide a standardized model for them. I have brought together such dissimilar hands because they are different from the other scripts of the de Gironcourt papers and because they share a peculiar trait that is absent in the other styles. In spite of the typical method of prolonging the final *sīn shīn*, *ṣād*, *ḍād*, *lām*, *nūn*, *yāʾ*, and *alif maqṣūrā* under the following word, thus creating an overlapping of words that is common in West Africa, the Masina manuscripts do not present this feature. All the words are clearly separated and uniformly, but tightly, distributed on the baseline. At this stage of analysis, it appears that Masina hands present some features common to what I call Central Sudanic cursive hands, as well as other characteristics that are linked to the *ṣaḥrāwī*.

The Sūqī

Among the scripts employed in the de Gironcourt papers, the most exemplary is the *sūqī* (figure 5). The *sūqī* is mainly the script of the Tuaregs[68] and takes its name from the Kel Es-Suq, the *ineslemen*[69] group which Harris T. Norris describes as the "masters" of this style.[70] Among the de Gironcourt manuscripts, the ones showing a *sūqī* are, in fact, mainly made by Kel Es-Suq scribes. However, specialists from other groups living in the eastern part of the Middle Niger (commonly used to refer to the region from Segou to the border of the modern states of Niger and Nigeria) also employ the *sūqī*: Tuareg of different tribal affiliation, Kunta, Fulani,

[68] Ḥammū, "Al-Kashf," 16.

[69] The *ineslemen* are the "religious class established after the introduction of Islam. In most Tuareg groups there are 'tribes' of *Ineslemen* under their own chiefs. Their status may vary from that of vassals to that of a status comparable with noble Tuaregs" (Harris T. Norris, *The Tuaregs: Their Islamic Legacy and Its Diffusion in the Sahel* [Warminster, Eng.: Aris and Phillips, 1975], 222, italics in the text.). De Moraes Farias describes the *ineslemen* as "specialists of Islam" (Paulo F. de Moraes Farias, *Arabic Medieval Inscriptions from the Republic of Mali: Epigraphy, Chronicles, and Songhay-Tuāreg History* [Oxford: Oxford University Press for the British Academy, 2003], xlv).

[70] Norris, *The Tuaregs*, 22.

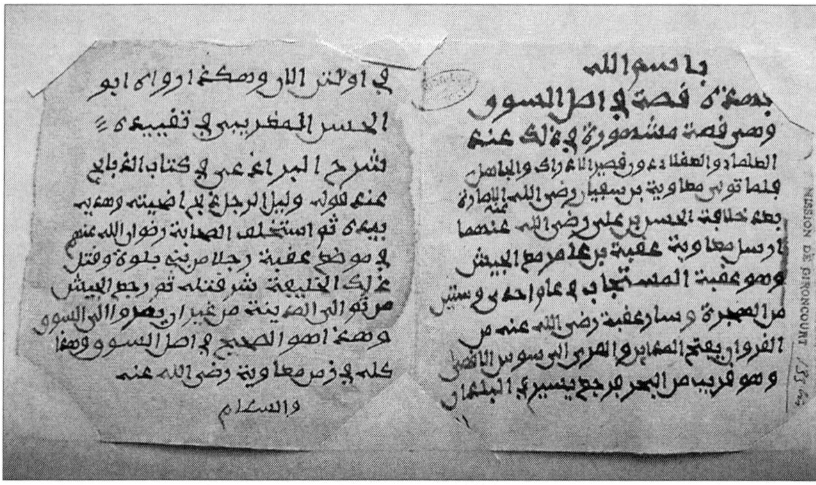

Figure 5.
Sūqī. De Gironcourt collection, ms. 2410 (133). History of the Kel Es-Suq. Copyist not mentioned (early twentieth century). Courtesy of Bibliothèque de l'Institut, Paris.

and Songhay. This suggests that non-Tuareg peoples living in the region touched by the Tuareg Sahelian diaspora equally adopted the *sūqī*.

Some scholars have suggested that the *sūqī* derives directly from the ancient script employed in the making of the West African epigraphs.[71] However, it is not easy to trace the development of this style back in time. All the manuscripts showing this script in the de Gironcourt collection date back only to 1911–12, like the rest of the collection, and I have not been able to find any dated manuscripts showing *sūqī* calligraphy in the secondary literature. While it is impossible, at the moment, to date the introduction and the spread of this style to a period prior to the early twentieth century, this does not imply that the *sūqī* could not have been used earlier.

My hypothesis is that the *sūqī* emerged as a peculiar script around the late seventeenth to the nineteenth centuries, along with the emergence of the social status of specialists of Islam for the Kel Es-Suq. Unfortunately,

[71] Norris, *The Tuaregs*, 22; Paulo F. de Moraes Farias, "The Oldest Extant Writing of West Africa: Medieval Epigraphs from Ɛssouk, Saney, and Egef-n-Tawaqqast (Mali)," *Journal de la Société des Africanistes* 60, no. 2 (1990): 85.

the question of when this status emerged is not easy to answer.[72] As Charles Grémont emphasizes, the Kel Es-Suq first appear in the sources at the beginning of the eighteenth century.[73] The scholar relies on the *Fatḥ al-shakūr* by the Walata scholar Muḥammad ʿAbd Allah al-Barṭīlī (d. 1805) to prove his hypothesis. In fact, it is from the eighteenth century that this biographical dictionary reports the first information about a scholar, a mystic expert of Qurʾanic sciences and *ḥadīths*, who bears a *nisba* related to the Kel Es-Suq, Aḥmad bin al-Bashīr al-Kalsūkī (d. 1770–71).[74] However, whether or not they were already recognized by the society as *ineslemen* is impossible to ascertain. De Moraes Farias suggests that the emergence of the Kel Es-Suq as specialists of Islam may have occurred in the late seventeenth century, after the dry seasons of the 1630s when they "must have faced with crucial negotiations of status" the Iwellemeden warriors.[75] An analysis of the sources shows that in the nineteenth century their status was firmly established.[76]

During the process of legitimization that established the Kel Es-Suq's status as Muslim specialists, a number of fictional traditions and genealogies were elaborated. Norris states that "the nomads among whom these *Ineslemen* were to minister needed some simple statement of 'history' which summarized their past and supplied an *apologia* in a few paragraphs."[77] Thus, the Saharan oral and written literature refers to the mythological figure of ʿUbqa al-Mustajāb as the ancestor of the Kel Es-Suq.[78] Traditions link some of them, the so-called *shurafāʾ*, to the Prophet, whereas others are associated with the people of Medina who allied with Muḥammad, the *anṣār*.[79] The core of such traditions is represented by the place from which all the Kel Es-Suq groups claim to originate: al-Sūq,

---

[72] Commenting on the general emergence of *ineslemen* status, Norris writes that "from documentary evidences it is not possible to give a date when this class was first integrated into Tuareg structure" (Norris, *The Tuaregs*, 20).

[73] Charles Grémont, *Les Touaregs Iwellemedan (1647–1896)* (Paris: Karthala, 2010), 95.

[74] Chouki El Hamel, trans., *La vie intellectuelle islamique dans le Sahel Ouest-africain (XVIe–XIXe siècles): Une étude sociale de l'enseignement islamique en Mauritanie et au Nord du Mali (XVIe–XIXe siècles) et traduction annotée de Fath ash-shakūr d'al-Bartilī al-Walātī (mort en 1805)* (Paris: Harmattan, 2002), 205–9.

[75] De Moraes Farias, *Arabic Medieval Inscriptions*, cxxxvii.

[76] See, for example, Heinrich Barth, *Travels and Discoveries in Northern and Central Africa* (New York: Harpers and Brothers, 1857), vol. 3, 459.

[77] Norris, *The Tuaregs*, 21.

[78] Ibid., 17–31.

[79] C. Grémont, *Les Touaregs*, 92.

the city identified with the Tadmakka recorded by Arab geographers.[80] It is from this city, located in the Adrar-des-Ifoghas Mountains, that the Kel Es-Suq take their name,[81] and it is here that the central "holy" elements of their traditions take root. Norris writes that

> [al-Sūq/Tadmakka] was a second Mecca to the Muslim Tuaregs. In their belief the sanctified hooves of the steed of ʿOqba [ʿUbqa], the Arab conqueror of Africa, had hallowed its sand and rock. The miraculous bones of the Prophet's Companions and Helpers had been interred in its graveyards.[82]

The ancient city of al-Sūq/Tadmakka was described in depth by Arab geographers, particularly by al-Bakrī in the mid-eleventh century, but it disappeared from the sources after the fifteenth century.[83] Local traditions ascribe to Sonni Ali, the Songhay emperor, the destruction of the city at the end of the fifteenth century.[84] Of the ancient splendor of al-Sūq/Tadmakka, nothing survives today, except for an amazing heritage of inscriptions carved in stone that are widespread on the site where the city was located.[85] The inscriptions present a simple unpointed Kufic, which de Moraes Farias dubs "Plain Sahelian Kufic," which, sometimes shows traces of ornaments changing to "Ǝssuk Ornamental Kufic."[86]

The aforementioned process of legitimization of the Kel Es-Suq status of *ineslemen* is also connected to their symbolic appropriation of the inscriptions, which constitute the main and characteristic physical vestige of the old al-Sūq/Tadmakka. However, instead of adopting the paleographic

---

[80] The association between the city of Tadmakka of the Arab geographers and the site of al-Sūq has been suggested for a long time by scholars. However, only in 2003, de Moraes Farias published an inscription proving that the names refer to the same place (Inscription no. 104, de Moraes Farias, *Arabic Medieval Inscriptions*, 87–88).

[81] In Tamashek, the name Kel Es-Suq corresponds to the Arab Ahl al-Sūq, meaning "the people of al-Sūq."

[82] Norris, *The Tuaregs*, 2.

[83] See Nehemia Levtzion and John F. P. Hopkins, eds., *Corpus of Early Arabic Sources for West African History* (Princeton: Markus Wiener, 2000); originally published by the Cambridge University Press in 1981.

[84] Barth, *Travels and Discoveries*, 458.

[85] In a crucial 2003 study, Paulo de Moraes Farias analyzed 77 inscriptions from al-Sūq/Tadmakka dated from 1013–14 to 1386 (de Moraes Farias, *Arabic Medieval Inscriptions*, 85–150).

[86] For a description of the script employed in al-Sūq inscriptions, see de Moraes Farias, *Arabic Medieval Inscriptions*, ccxxxi–ccliii.

style of the inscriptions, the Kel Es-Suq realized a new, markedly Kufic style, the *sūqī*, which though not ancient, is specifically designed to be perceived as archaic and monumental. In Saharan Africa this practice of creating archaic scripts is not an isolated case. According to Théodore Monod, who analyzes the process by studying other Central Sudanic epigraphs, it gives birth to a form of "*conservatisme graphique.*"[87]

The *sūqī*'s paleographic characteristics resemble the Kufic, and the script is characterized by the angularity of its letters.

- The letters *dāl* and *dhāl*, *ʿayn* and *ghayn* (isolated and initial), and *kāf* are markedly hooked;
- The *alif*, *lām*, *bāʾ*, *tāʾ*, and *thāʾ* (initial and isolated) and *nūn* and *yāʾ* (initial), as well as the diagonal stem of the *ṭāʾ* and *ẓāʾ*, often present a hook at the top. *Hāʾ* (isolated) and *tāʾ marbūṭa* present a similarly hooked stem;
- It is not always easy to differentiate *ṣād* and *mīm*, which are distinguishable only by their size. They are both made, as well as the *ṣād* and *ḍād*, with a nearly perpendicular right stroke and a semi-loop that develops towards the left. In the same way are drawn the letters *qāf* and *fāʾ*, but the semi-loop is usually less elongated;
- Medial and final *ʿayn* and *ghayn* show an unusual tooth at the left top;
- Initial and medial *hāʾ* is written as two adjacent triangles. Sometimes its angular form may acquire a rounder shape or even resemble an "8," with the longer side lying on the baseline and flattened on it. The first of the two sections of the letter may be left unclosed or even unconnected;
- *Alif* is sometimes written in a bent fashion;
- The stroke of the letters *rāʾ* and *zāʾ*, as well as the right one of the *wāw*, forms an obtuse angle of about 135° on the line. The page appears in this way, characterized by three well-defined sets of lines: the baselines, the vertical lines over which letters like medial *lām*, *alif*, and *bāʾ* teeth, etc., are drawn, and the diagonal one formed by the lower section of *rāʾ*, *zāʾ* and *wāw*.

Below is a complete alphabet of the standard *sūqī* script, including the peculiar form of the couple *lām-alif*, the preposition *fī*, and the name of God (*Allāh*).

---

[87] Théodore Monod, "Sur les inscriptions arabes peintes de Ti-m-Missao (Sahara central)," *Journal de la Société des Africanistes* 8, no. 1 (1938): 94.

Final	Medial	Initial	Isolated	Name of the letter
ـا	ـا	ا	ا	alif
ـب ـت ـث	ـبـ ـتـ ـثـ	بـ تـ ثـ	ب ت ث	baʾ, tāʾ, thāʾ
ـج ـح ـخ	ـجـ ـحـ ـخـ	جـ حـ خـ	ج ح خ	jīm, ḥaʾ, lhāʾ
ـد ـذ	ـد ـذ	د ذ	د ذ	dāl, dhāl
ـر ـز	ـر ـز	ر ز	ر ز	rāʾ, zāʾ
ـس ـش	ـسـ ـشـ	سـ شـ	س ش	sīn, shīn
ـص ـض	ـصـ ـضـ	صـ ضـ	ص ض	ṣād, ÿād
ـط ـظ	ـطـ ـظـ	طـ ظـ	ط ظ	ṭāʾ, ẓāʾ
ـع ـغ	ـعـ ـغـ	عـ غـ	ع غ	ʿayn, ghayn
ـڢ	ـڢـ	ڢـ	ڢ	fāʾ
ـڧ	ـڧـ	ڧـ	ڧ	qāf
ـك	ـكـ	كـ	ك	kāf
ـل	ـلـ	لـ	ل	lām
ـم	ـمـ	مـ	م	mīm
ـن	ـنـ	نـ	ن	nūn

Final	Medial	Initial	Isolated	Name of the letter
				*ha* (*tāʾ marbuṭa*)
				wāw
				*yāʾ*
-	-	-		*hamza*
-	-	-	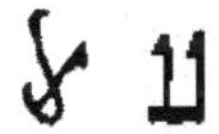	(*lām-alif*)
-	-	-		(*fī*)
-	-	-		(*Allāh*)

Conclusion

This paper has emphasized that our knowledge of West African writing styles is unsatisfying and that precise labels to define the different scripts employed in the region are missing. However, the contributions of West African scholars on this topic have added new input to this field of study. Starting from their research, this paper has identified five categories of scripts employed in the manuscripts of the de Gironcourt collection: *ṣaḥrāwī*, *maghribī*, *sūqī*, Central Sudanic cursive hands, and Masina hands.

The study of these categories suggests the existence of regional variations of writing styles instead of ethnic ones, as usually advanced in the literature on the topic. The case of the *sūqī* supports this hypothesis. The paper suggests that the *sūqī* emerged among the *ineslemen* Kel Es-Suq, but was also employed by scribes of different tribal or ethnic affiliation living in the eastern middle Niger, an area deeply influenced by the Tuareg diaspora. Moreover, the cases of the *ṣaḥrāwī*, employed in a wide Sahelo-Saharan zone from Mauritania to Timbuktu, and that of the Central

Sudanic cursive hands, prove that traditions of writing styles cross ethnic and tribal boundaries and have to be treated as regional phenomena.

A further remark concerns the historical depth of distribution of the writing styles advanced by this paper. The analysis of three of the eighteenth- and nineteenth-century documents[88] offers interesting suggestions concerning the unfolding of West African writing styles through time. The ms. 2416 (211)/I, a copy of the *Naṣīḥat ahl al-zamān* by the "Nigerian" *mujāhid* ʿUthmān b. Fodiye (d. 1817), was copied in the mid-nineteenth century by Ibrāhīm al-Khalīl, son of ʿAbd Allāh bin Fūdī and first emir of Gwandu (r. 1835–60).[89] The script of the manuscript differs substantially from the more recent northern Nigerian style, resembling the *jihādī/ṣaḥrāwī*. However, Bivar proposes that this script developed during the revolutionary movement of ʿUthmān b. Fodiye, whereas the de Gironcourt manuscripts suggests that such a style already existed. The manuscript 2414 (200)/I is a copy dating to 1769 of the *Taʾrīkh al-Sūdān*, the well-known chronicle by ʿAbd al-Raḥmān al-Saʿdī.[90] This manuscript was found in Sokoto by the above-mentioned Ibrāhīm al-Khalīl, but unfortunately it does not report information on its place of realization. The script found in this manuscript is also very close to the *jihādī/ṣaḥrāwī*. This notion problematizes the pertinence of the label *jihādī* employed by Bivar, considering that the existence of this style is attested before 1804, the date usually evoked as the beginning of ʿUthmān b. Fodiye's movement. Thus, in my opinion the label *ṣaḥrāwī* is to be preferred to *jīhādī*.

The existence of such a style in the region of Timbuktu is also attested in the nineteenth-century manuscript 2407 (121). It is a copy of the *Kitāb al-Tarāʾif* by Muḥammad bin al-Mukhtār al-Kuntī (d. 1825–26), presumably an autograph, according to a suggestion by de Gironcourt.

Thus it appears that the *ṣaḥrāwī* was widespread in West Africa in the nineteenth century, from Nigeria to Timbuktu. While in the Nigerian region it was replaced by a new style during the nineteenth century, it remains the preferred scripts of the people of the Sahelo-Saharian region of Mali and Mauritania. It is possible to propose tentatively that this style appeared in this northern region of West Africa, maybe in the ancient towns

[88] The fourth oldest manuscript (ms. 2416 (121)/I) has been excluded from this analysis because it was made by the British consul in Tripoli, G. F. Herman, so it does not reflect any West African tradition.

[89] Nobili, "'Rediscovering' the de Gironcourt Collection," 59.

[90] Ibid., 59.

of Walata and Timbuktu, which were among the ancient centers for the spread of Islam and Islamic culture in West Africa and whose links to the Maghreb are well attested in the sources.[91]

However, the analysis of the styles displayed in the de Gironcourt manuscripts shows traces of another influence on the development of regional scripts, especially with regard to Central Sudanic cursive hands. Such an influence may derive from Bornu, an important center of West African Islamic culture, which according to Bivar gave birth to a characteristic writing style.

Thus, this paper proposes a model of development of West African scripts that includes two separate areas for the original elaboration of writing styles: the ancient Islamic centers of the Mauritanian and Malian Sahelo-Saharian belt, and Bornu. Following this model, Masina, which is strongly related to both such centers, produced a style that balances their influences.[92]

Finally, the case of the *sūqī* lies outside this model. The script emerged sometime between the early seventeenth century and the middle of the nineteenth century and it stands out as an eccentric case study, because it is related to the establishment of the *ineslemen* status of the Kel Es-Suq.

[91] The link of this region with North Africa is attested in the sources since the years of the empire of Mali (see Nehemia Levtzion, *Ancient Ghana and Mali* [London: Methuen, 1973], 213–17). The *Ta'rīkh al-sūdān* mentions that since the early thirteenth century, scholars from Timbuktu were going to Fez to study (John O. Hunwick, *Timbuktu and the Songhay Empire: Al-Sa'dīs Ta'rīkh al-Sūdān down to 1613 and Other Contemporary Documents* [Leiden: Brill, 2003], 81).

[92] See, for example, Charles C. Stewart, "Frontier Disputes and Problems of Legitimations: Sokoto–Masina Relations 1817–1837," *Journal of African History* 17, no. 4 (1976).

BOOK REVIEWS

Fadlalla, Amal Hassan. *Embodying Honor: Fertility, Foreignness, and Regeneration in Eastern Sudan.* Madison: University of Wisconsin Press, 2007. Women in Africa and the Diaspora, Stanlie James and Aili Mari Tripp, series editors. 240 pp., glossary, 25 black-and-white photographs and an eight-page color insert, 4 tables, and 1 map. $55.00

This richly detailed ethnography examines the multiple challenges to women's fertility among a group of Muslim Hadendowa migrants to the informal settlement on the edge of Sinkat in eastern Sudan, and how these women understand and act to maintain their group identity in the face of enormous political and socioeconomic change. Fadlalla's study adds a useful dimension to our understanding of women's reproductive struggles as part of a larger community effort to cope with local and global power relations. Illustrating the ideal of "responsible motherhood" through an astute analysis of gendered notions of morality and respectability, the author uses women's narratives to understand their lifetime strategies for healthy reproduction. Central to this understanding is the representation of "foreignness," a cultural concept rooted in a historical narrative that is used to explain and respond to potential threats from "outside." Fadlalla's rather complex and dense analysis nevertheless paints a compelling picture of Hadendowa women's social and bodily management of their fertility in relation to the "regeneration" of their community through reference to a particular complex of foreignness.

Islamic Africa, VOL. 1, NO. 1, 2010. ISSN 2154-0993. www.islamicafricajournal.org

Embodying Honor is organized into six chapters. These develop the author's narrative from an overview of the political economy of the Hadendowa in historical context to a highly detailed analysis of women's honor and morality (*durarit,* in Tu-Badawie) in strategizing responsible motherhood and coping with reproductive suffering. Using the narratives of women as a starting point, Fadlalla weaves her own observations and experiences into the chapters, giving the reader a rich ethnographic understanding of Hadendowa gender expectations, religious practices, spatial arrangements and tent construction, food preparation and taboos, bodily adornment and comportment, ritual practices and the spirit world, and a host of other social and cultural practices and beliefs. The concept of *auslif,* parsed as those familiar with and the habitual practices derived from "the legacy of the ancestors and the power of the Qurʾan, hadith (the Prophet's sayings), and the baraka of religious saints and healers" (12) is contrasted with that which is considered "foreign." Fadlalla makes clear that this apparent dichotomy is, in actual practice, fuzzy and subject to shifts of meaning on both sides—as in the strategic receptiveness of some of the younger women to Islamic trends of understanding and treating infertility (166–67). That is, while new patterns of *auslif* are incorporated into tackling infertility, successful reproductive trajectories (leading to the birth of sons) assert Hadendowa women's centrality in the social regeneration of their group.

We find out a range of pertinent information about the precarious livelihoods and structural injustice of Hadendowa as their nomadic way of life was increasingly incorporated into the Sudanese state. As a Muslim non-Arabic-speaking minority, the Hadendowa were marginalized through state-centered development processes that eventually compromised their access to grazing rights and fomented conflict with neighboring or competing groups. These and other pressures led to displacement and forced urbanization in the provincial towns of eastern Sudan and to the Hadendowa's introduction to the world of humanitarian relief. It is fascinating to be led along the pathway of understanding through the eyes of the author, a Sudanese anthropologist who is constructed by her Hadendowa research participants as *balaweit,* or northern Sudanese. Through this experiential lens, Fadlalla learns about the ways in which this identity also implies "foreigner, intruder, and superior," and from there gains insight into the complex relationship Hadendowa have to "foreignness," and the ambiguous role of Islam implied by this. It is from these insights that Fadlalla draws her understanding of the threat not only to group identity but to the health, well-being, and fertility of Hadendowa women. Managing their fertility—and especially "son-fertility," which solidifies women's roles not only as responsible mothers but also as ritual leaders—is crucial for the continued maintenance and renewal of the Hadendowa people.

These interrelated insights make for a fascinating analysis that claims to bring a political economy dimension to fertility and reproductive events at the family (micro) and population (macro) levels. Fadlalla's observation of Hadendowa women's pervasive commentary on their social vulnerability in the way they narrated their own reproductive struggles is key to understanding women's recognition of broader inequalities and also of their agency in the face of injustice and personal and social suffering. The ethnographic detail Fadlalla weaves into her presentation of Hadendowa women's lives gives the reader a soberingly comprehensive picture of their experiences of miscarriages, stillbirths, and health crises that compromise their ideal reproductive trajectories.

It is this level of comprehensiveness on Hadendowa health and fertility that, in my view, detracts somewhat from the broader argument that the author has outlined so convincingly at the outset of her book. While "foreignness" is a central theme in women's explanations about their own suffering and a metaphor for threats from "outside," one gets only a vague sense of the Hadendowa's actual interaction with the exterior world. It would have been extremely useful to have additional day-to-day context within which to site women's narratives about their reproductive trajectories. The short final chapter, in which the new reality of Hadendowa urban lives is briefly described, comes quite late in the book to help us make sense of the transformed political economy of fertility as narrated by women themselves. In terms of readability, while the book's overall structure—its nested chapters and clear subheadings—is elegant, I found the text itself hard to follow. There is a wide use of Tu-Badawie words but no clear rationale for which of these convey specific cultural meaning and which are merely everyday terms, necessitating more (in my view) flipping back and forth to the glossary than is strictly necessary. The writing is somewhat choppy, lurching uncomfortably between richly detailed ethnographic description and obtuse theoretical language. Finally, the author seems to pursue an everything-but-the-kitchen-sink approach to her ethnographic data —fine, but for the theoretical objectives stated at the outset to move the anthropological lens beyond bodily experiences and local representations of reproduction and child-rearing.

Fadlalla's goal to propel the medical anthropology and population literature on women's own understanding of their fertility into a broader sociopolitical framework is laudable, and the book succeeds in making a case for why this is relevant and necessary. However, including more data on Hadendowa accommodation or adaptation to their contemporary urban situation would help the reader to understand the draw of "traditional" practices to address their current vulnerability more fully.

Anita Fábos, Clark University

Sean Hanretta, *Islam and Social Change in French West Africa: History of an Emancipatory Community.* Cambridge, UK: Cambridge University Press, 2009. 305 + xv pp.; glossary, index, bibliography, 3 maps, and 5 black-and-white illustrations.

Two ghosts hover over Sean Hanretta's *Islam and Social Change in French West Africa.* They are the traces of two men who died in obscure circumstances in French provinces or borderlands in the opening years of the Second World War, one a refugee, the other a prisoner. The Marxism of the iconoclastic Jewish critic Walter Benjamin was every bit as fundamentally heterodox as Shaykh Ahmed Hamallah's particular path within the Tijaniyya, at least within the doctrines of the moment. Although one would be hard pressed to think of what else the two men might have had in common, each in their own way produced a clutch of powerful ideas that resonated with brilliant and ambitious disciples.

Few historians of Islam—or indeed of Africa—owe as much to Benjamin as Hanretta does. By the same token, perhaps none of the other West African shaykhs who rose to prominence in the twentieth century had a relationship with his own spiritual master that was simultaneously as intense and as idiosyncratic as that between Hamallah and Yacouba Sylla, whose teachings and the community they engendered are at the core of this book. Every bit as iconoclastic as his spiritual master, Yacouba Sylla never claimed to figure among the ulema of the Western Sahel. He simply rejected some of their teachings, especially around the question of marriage and dowries, while seeking to mitigate the inequalities that then characterized Sahelian societies. In the 1920s and '30s this message generated controversy, but it won him a following of ex-slaves and others of low social status, among whom figured more women than men. Claiming a unique and direct relationship with Hamallah, himself a controversial figure and the object of colonial repression, Sylla invoked the ire of his elders and his preaching helped provoke communal violence, most notably in the Mauritanian town of Kaedi in 1930. Exiled to the Côte d'Ivoire by the French administration, he would build a new community of Muslims there. In the Sahel, Sylla had received the gift of Hamallah's blessing, a gift he believed his shaykh had in turn received from Ahmad al-Tijani and, therefore, from the Prophet himself. In the Ivorian town of Gagnoa, he passed that gift along, transforming it into the basis of a tightly knit, ostensibly egalitarian, virtually endogamous, and aggressively entrepreneurial community of Muslims with its geographic base in the southern Côte d'Ivoire. Adapting to exile, Sylla and his followers left the Sahel behind. Even if Soninke remains the ritual language of Yacouba Sylla's community, the shaykh's relations with prominent members of the Hamawiyya in Nioro-du-Sahel were tense, and the Côte d'Ivoire became his home. In the immediate postwar years, he began to build a strong relationship with the planter, politician, and future president Félix Houphouët-Boigny. Until the shaykh's death in 1988, his worldly fortunes rose with that of his adopted country. This story, in its broad outlines, occupies most of parts 1 and 3 of Hanretta's book. Contrasting the colonial library, broadly construed, with a view of "History in the *Zâwiya,*" part 2 asks how we can know what we think we do, and how we might begin to interpret it.

In a work that braids intellectual and social history, Hanretta argues for a "weak" contextualization that displaces colonial rule from the center of historical analysis, adopting in its place a "*longue durée*" view of the arc of West African Muslim history. For Hanretta, inscribing Yacouba Sylla within that long arc means loosening the interpretive bonds that tie him and his community to a certain colonial moment and to a particular political economy. The gambit is clear. Hanretta builds on Benjamin's trenchant critiques of a once-prevalent form of historicism to offer a defense of history-writing as a humanistic exercise, one in which (crudely put) neither structure nor agency is determinant. This approach requires simultaneously and rigorously understanding Yacouba Sylla's community both on its own terms and as representative of something larger. Welcome as it is, it is not without risks. Let me suggest two. First, it is hard to avoid the impression that modernity and its variants may be a more significant category to the historian and his theorist than to the adepts and their shaykh. Second, Sylla's apparent disinterest in the work of the ulema, which bordered on anti-intellectualism, stands out rather sharply against the deep background of West African Muslim history. Does "loose contextualization" preclude further explanation?

Drawn from Paul Klee's painting "Angelus Novus," Benjamin's best-known metaphor is not a simple one: the angel of history, propelled forward by the winds of progress but with his back turned towards the future, looks in horror at the receding but ever-expanding "catastrophe" of the past.[1] Although we might name them differently, the winds that blew in Sylla's time were exceedingly strong. In this rich and intellectually ambitious work, Hanretta guides us toward their identification.

Gregory Mann, Columbia University

Ousseina D. Alidou, *Engaging Modernity: Muslim Women and the Politics of Agency in Postcolonial Niger*. Madison: University of Wisconsin Press, 2005. 235 + xxi pp.; ill., 9 tables, 2 appendices, index, bibliography.

In recent years, exploring the intersection of gender and modernity in Muslim societies has assumed a certain urgency. At a time when Islamic reformism is uncritically assumed by some to lead to the sweeping homogenization of the Muslim world, tracing the distinctions between men's and women's understanding of Islam is one of the avenues through which scholars can complicate the notion of an increasingly uniform Muslim tradition. This is precisely what Ousseina Alidou set out to do in her engaging study of Muslim women in fin-de-siècle Niger. By documenting how some Nigerien women have successfully carved a place for themselves in the changing religious economy, Alidou recovers the "alternative voice of women" (156), illuminating in the process how the experience of modernity is shaped by local ideas of gender, morality, and agency.

Alidou's concern is to demonstrate that, far from being pawns in the political and religious games played by their male counterparts, Nigerien women have agency. After witnessing women's active contribution to the socioeconomic and religious life of Niamey, Alidou, a linguist and

[1] Walter Benjamin, "Ninth Thesis on the Philosophy of History," in *Illuminations,* ed. Hannah Arendt, trans. Harry Zohn (New York: Schocken Books, 1986). Along the same lines, Hanretta's copy editor might look in horror at the missing footnotes on page 60.

cultural critic by training, decided to explore female activism through a focus on the lives of three women. Malama Aʾishatu is a Qurʾanic teacher and an Islamic expert whose religious commentaries and poetry are routinely broadcast on the radio and television. Habsu Garba is a renowned singer-dancer and an entertainer for what was until recently the country's ruling political party. Agaisha (a pseudonym) is a successful political activist who served as the voice of Tuareg women's liberation during the conflict that opposed Tuareg populations to the Nigerien government. Each of these women successfully rose to prominence by forging a hybrid professional life against the backdrop of political, economic, and religious reforms that powerfully impacted women's capacity for self-definition and empowerment.

By tracing their biographies, Alidou highlights the contours of women's agency, which she defines, following Judith Butler and Saba Mahmood, as a capacity for action that arises out of specific conditions of subordination. Thus it was precisely because she was denied access to French education that Malama Aʾishatu fought to attend Qurʾanic school—a move that would have profound consequences for her future career as a Muslim religious leader. Similarly Habsu Garba had to defy social conventions to establish herself as a performing artist. For Agaisha, it was the very war that victimized her as a "native" woman that provided the possibility for self-empowerment when her local world was turned upside down. Through their efforts to educate young girls, participate in family planning, or mediate peace agreements, these three women have visibly and actively contributed to the reconfiguration of the social landscape. Particularly compelling for this reader was Alidou's insistence that Nigerien women's activism be set against the backdrop of *brassage Sahélien,* a process of ethnic and cultural mixing that has heightened the irrelevance of ethnicity as an analytical category. By adopting a trans-ethnic approach to examine women's experience of Islam and modernity, Alidou successfully captures the complexity of women's identities while contributing valuable insights to the study of gender and ethnicity.

In Niger the democratization movement, the rise of religious reformism, and the economic decline triggered by structural adjustment programs have provoked a "realignment of the space of men and women" (19). While this realignment has hampered the development of certain forms of female agency, it has encouraged others. In this new space of possibilities Alidou explores how, by negotiating the rules governing their mobility, their visibility, as well as their sense of agentive personhood, women have gained a sharper sense of what it means to be Muslim and modern. The analysis is enriched by Alidou's reflections as a "native" woman, particularly her own experience of growing up in Niger. Whether she discusses girl's and women's education, the politics of language, or the role of the media in the articulation of women's subjectivities, Alidou does a good job of tracing the gendered tensions that emerge as women develop a new awareness of themselves and of their rights.

Aʾishatu, Habsu, and Agaisha, it is important to note, are elite women. Although they had to overcome strong biases and work hard to establish themselves as women in their respective fields, they nonetheless belong to a privileged minority who enjoys the benefits of education and economic independence. As such they cannot be said to represent Nigerien women who, for the most part, are poor, unschooled, and economically dependent on male kin. Alidou's celebration of Nigerien women's agency sounds a bit emphatic when set against the lives of countless ordinary women in Niamey and elsewhere for whom "self-empowerment" has a distinctly different connotation. By the same token, her insistence that "patriarchy defines most Nigerien ethnic and cultural practices" (184) needs to be further nuanced. Simply defining practices as "patriarchal" does not illuminate the roots of women's conditions, nor does it contribute to an understanding of how women themselves (save for a few educated ones) see the terms of their exclusion from a world of possibilities. Chapter 4, in which Alidou analyzes a fairy tale narrated by Habsu Garba on the national radio, feels out of place in part because it is not sufficiently contextualized. The narrative, a Hausa version of Cinderella, is interpreted by Alidou as "a tale of liberation in which women's agency over their destiny and their triumph over oppression is evident" (145). While no one would quibble with Alidou over the fact that Cinderella is a story about the triumph of kindness and integrity over oppression, I would nonetheless caution against a hasty reading informed by liberal discourses on women's liberation.

These criticisms do not diminish Alidou's significant contribution to the scholarship on women in Africa. *Engaging Modernity* is an enjoyable book to read, not the least because it is full of wonderful anecdotes and insights on the ways that the "woman question" is being debated in the Nigerien public and private spheres. It is also a compelling study that sheds light on how some Muslim women have created for themselves a space of self-determination within the constraints that are imposed on them.

Adeline Masquelier, Tulane University

Becker, Felicitas. *Becoming Muslim in Mainland Tanzania, 1890–2000.* A British Academy postdoctoral fellowship monograph. Oxford: Oxford University Press, 2008. 364 pp.; ill., glossary, bibliography, index. $100.

This monograph offers an engaging reconstruction of the adoption and practice of Islam among villagers in southeastern Tanzania from the end of the nineteenth century to the present, focusing on "relationships between the coast and the countryside *from the rural end*" (9). The author accounts for villagers' conversion to Islam by tracing processes of simultaneous forms of religious change, the transmission and acquisition of knowledge, and the adoption of new identities and changing social relations in a post-abolitionary context. Situating these processes within a changing political and economic framework, she provides a historical background to Islamic practices, reform movements, education, gender relations, and Muslims' relations to political authorities in present times. With individual chapters discussing these themes partly chronologically and partly thematically, this monograph appeals to a diverse, interdisciplinary audience: those interested in a regional history of southeastern Tanzania and in understanding processes of Islamization and social relations in Muslim societies more generally, and those trying to gain insight into the interaction between the interior and the East African coast within the context of wider Indian Ocean networks.

The author has drawn on a wide range of sources to offer an account which focuses on local actors within a trans-local framework. She conducted hundreds of interviews over a period of seven years to generate answers to her main research questions, such as how villagers in southeastern Tanzania adopted Islam during the first half of the twentieth century, and which individual needs they pursued by converting or adding new religious elements to existing ones. Her focus on oral history, which allows her to suggest how the actors experienced the adoption of Islam and how their reasons and choices of incorporating Islam changed during the twentieth century, is convincingly complemented by governmental and missionary records, and a wide range of secondary sources.

Becker's primary sources lead her to highlight the local relevance of Islam to maintaining and improving social relations. She argues that when individuals adopted new religious forms, they bargained for creating new power constellations between genders and generations, whereby she stresses the actors' conscious decisions about which elements and forms of Islam to adopt. Throughout the volume, the author highlights the compatibility of maintaining established practices and introducing religious change. The realms of healing and reconciliation, in which Islamic forms complemented existing practices rather than radically replaced them, constitute examples of historical continuity, whereas the construction of Quranic schools and mosques created new foci of social life, representing a break from precolonial practice (82).

The author starts her account by pointing to the previously ignored paradox that in her region of study, conversion to Islam increased during the initially German and then British colonial period, and thus after the peak of Omani influence from Zanzibar and the collapse of long-distance trade (4–5). She explains this peculiarity by pointing to two interacting processes: the adoption of Islam by non-Muslims in rural areas and the spread of Sufi orders in and their focus on urban areas which already featured a Muslim population (5–6). Drawing on her vast body of interviews, she argues that the adaptability or "polyvalence"of Islam enabled its continuous appeal to villagers in southeastern Tanzania. She demonstrates that after 1920 exclusive, hierarchical forms of Islam, tied to slavery and the long-distance trade, shifted to inclusive, egalitarian ones. In the interwar period, the appeal of Islam changed from enabling struggle for citizenship and socioeconomic participation to becoming a "ritual and intellectual experiment" (83), broadening one's worldview. Facilitated by shifting power relations during colonial rule, the actors had changed by the 1930s, when rural Muslims were "ordinary villagers rather than big men" (68). She thus provides new evidence for the argument developed by Jonathon Glassman in his study on the Mrima coast that changing power relations (initiated, for instance, by the collapse of the long-distance trade and colonial rule) could be redressed by changing religious practices, such as by incorporating Islamic ones.

Given the ambitious chronological and thematic scope of this monograph, the conclusion offers a welcome reminder of some of the main themes and arguments developed by the author: the relationship between religious ritual and negotiations of social relations; the dichotomy between the knowledgeable and the ignorant manifest in Islamic thought; gender and intergenerational relations; the distribution of religious affiliations; town-countryside relations and by extension local and global Islam; Islamic modernity and the *Ansar Sunna*, as well as Islamic radicalism. On a conceptual level, Becker contributes to the increasingly prolific literature on modernity in Africa. Her work shows that in the 1930s the appeal of the coast to rural villagers represented a form of locally defined modernity, with rural actors aiming to participate in wider Swahili and Indian Ocean networks (112–13). Notions of modernity are further exemplified in exploring the reformist group *Ansar Sunna*, operating locally since the late 1970s, their relations to the state, and their contradictory approach towards the West and non-Muslims.

One of Becker's categories of analysis, gender, is addressed as far as sources allowed, yet would have benefited from further elaboration to make clear transformations in gender relations, particularly the religiously induced shift from matrilineage to patrilineage during the twentieth century (e.g., 149). Some of her arguments confirm our current understanding that the most significant changes in gender relations along the Swahili coast in the twentieth century were induced by the abolition of slavery and by Sufi orders that enabled women's participation in Islamic rituals. She further adds evidence to our understanding that in urban areas patrician ideals restricted women's economic activities, while husbands at the lower end of the socioeconomic ladder imitated these ideals and thereby limited the previous scope of their wives' agency (284). This concurs with findings across the Muslim world that rural women have been less restrained by ideal notions of socioeconomic behavior, thus emphasizing a divide in practicing Islam between urban and rural communities. Becker's suggestion that adopting Islam enabled villagers "to restate a gendered separation of the domestic and public spheres that had lost some of its practical significance with the end of the threat of enslavement" (110) is intriguing, and would become more tangible if evidenced further.

In this rich regional study, Becker offers a captivating and nuanced interpretation of conversion to Islam, which places the role of coastal Muslim traders in an ambiguous light and defines the agency and choices of local rulers and villagers as driven by various factors, such as participation in interregional networks, and redefining social rights and obligations manifest in rituals and access to knowledge. As the author suggests, the actors' bargaining for participation continued in "a quiet appropriation of citizenship in the Indian Ocean region" (112) after independence. Navigating between continuity and change, this monograph challenges notions of the urbanity of Islam on the Swahili coast. It increases our understanding of the complex interactions between coast and interior and locates the rural actors more firmly within Islamic networks in the western Indian Ocean.

Elke E. Stockreiter, University of Iowa